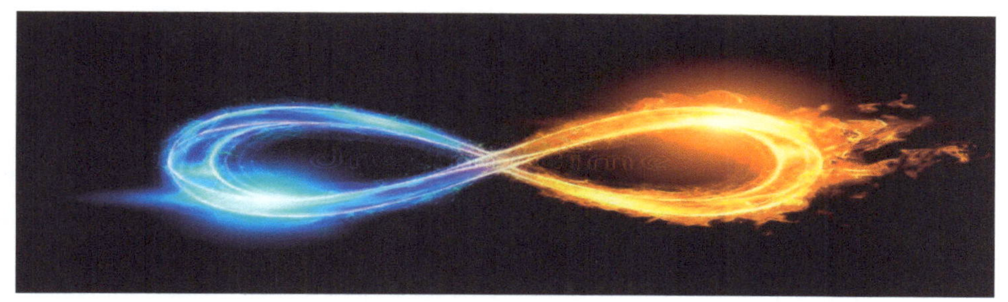

IN SEARCH OF GOD

(Version 1.0)
(A compilation and commentary)

By GOPALA KRISHNA MERUVA

Foreword

The first of the seven Universal Laws tells us that "The All is Mind - The Universe is Conscious". Everything we see and experience is our physical world has its origin in the invisible, conscious realm. it tells us that there is a single Universal - The Universal Mind - from which all things manifest. All energy and matter at all levels is created by and is subordinate to the Omnipresent Universal Mind. Our mind is part of the Universal Mind- the same in kind with the only difference being one of degree. Our reality is a manifestation of our mind.

<u>Topics</u>

1. The Hindu Model of this Universe

2. What is the Purpose of Creation

3. The Western Model of this Universe

4. Un answered Questions/Mysteries

CHAPTER 1

<u>The Hindu Model of Multiverse</u>

VEDIC HINDU COSMOLOGY

In ancient Hindu Cosmology, what we know as the Earth is only one of countless worlds located in Brahmanda, which is itself only one of the unconutable universes. The known world was located in the middle of Bhu-loka, comprised of many ring-shaped landmasses separated by oceans of various composition. From its center rose Mount Meru, reaching into the heavens. With the cycle of reincarnation, it was possible to reach other, upper or lower realms (or lokas). Below the Bhu-loka was a multitude of increasingly worse hellish realms, with the ocean Garbhodaka located at the very bottom. Above the Earth and the sky were the heavenly realms, with the abode of the creator god Brahma located at the top of the world.

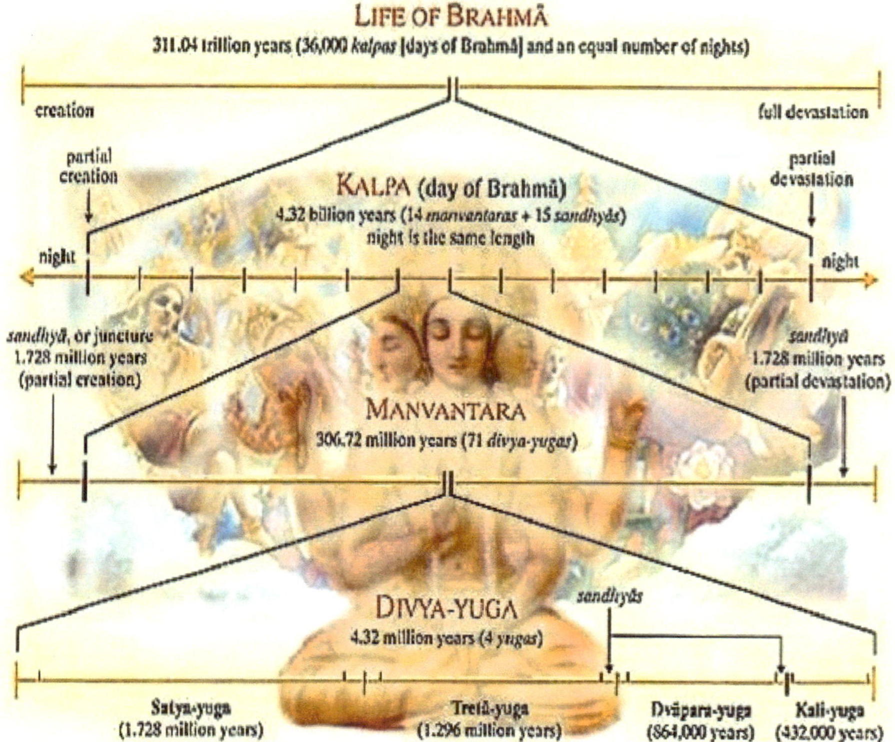

According to Hindu vedic cosmology, there is no absolute start to time, as it is considered infinite and cyclic.Similarly, the space and universe has neither start nor end, rather it is cyclical.The current universe is just the start of a present cycle pre- ceded by an infinite number of universes and to be followed by another infinite number of universes.The dominant theme in Puranic Hindu cosmology state ,Chap- man and Driver, is of cycles and repetition.There are multiple universes, each takes birth from chaos, grows, decays and dies into chaos, to be reborn again. Further, there are different and parallel realities.

One complete cycle of the four (Kr ta or Satya, Treta, Dvapara and Kali) Yugas is one Mahā-Yuga (4.32 million solar years) and is confirmed by the Gītā Śloka 8.17 (statement) "sahasra-yuga-paryantam ahar yad brahmaṇo viduḥ rātrim yuga-sahasrāntām te 'ho-rātra-vido janāḥ", meaning, a day of brahma is of 1000 Mahā- Yuga. Rigveda: speculation on universe's creationThe Rigveda which is variously dated, generally in the second half of the 2nd-millennium BCE,presents many theories of cosmology.

For example:

Hiranyagarbha sukta, its hymn 10.121, states a golden child was born in the universe and was the lord, established earth and heaven, then asks but who is the god to whom we shall offer the sacrificial prayers?Devi sukta, its hymn 10.125, states a goddess is all, the creator, the created universe, the feeder and the lover of the universe;Nasadiya sukta, its hymn 10.129, asks who created the universe, does anyone really know, and whether it can ever be known.According to Henry White Wallis, the Rigveda and other Vedic texts are full of alternative cosmological theories and curiosity questions. For example, the hymn 1.24 of the Rigveda asks, "these stars, which are set on high, and appear at night, whither do they go in the daytime?"

and hymn 10.88 wonders, "how many fires are there, how many suns, how many dawns, how many waters? I am not posing an awkward question for you fathers; I ask you, poets, only to find out?"

To its numerous open-ended questions, the Vedic texts present a diversity of thought, in verses imbued with symbols and allegory, where in some cases forces and agencies are clothed with a distinct personality, while in other cases as nature with or without anthropomorphic activity such as forms of mythical sacrifices.The Rigveda contains the Nasadiya sukta hymn which does not offer a cosmological theory, but asks cosmological questions about the nature of universe and how it began:Darkness there was at first, by darkness hidden; Without distinctive marks, this all was water; That which, becoming, by the void was covered; That One by force of heat came into being;

Deborah Soifer describes the development of the concept of lokas as follows:The concept of a loka or lokas develops in the Vedic literature. Influenced by the special connotations that a word for space might have for a nomadic people, loka in the Veda did not simply mean place or world, but had a positive valuation: it was a place or position of religious or psychological interest with a special value of function of its own. Hence, inherent in the 'loka' concept in the earliest literature was a double aspect; that is, coexistent with spatiality was a religious meaning, which could exist independent of a spatial notion, an 'immaterial' significance. The most common cosmological conception of lokas in the Veda was that of the triple world: three worlds consisting of earth, atmosphere or sky, and heaven, making up the universe."The Puranas genre of Indian literature, found in Hinduism and Jainism, contain a section on cosmology and cosmogony as a requirement. There are dozens of different Mahapuranas and Upapuranas, each with its own theory integrated into a proposed human history consisting of solar and lunar dynasties. Some are similar to Indo-European creation myths, while others are novel. One cosmology, shared by Hindu, Buddhist and Jain texts involves Mount Meru, with stars and sun moving around it using Dhruva (North Star) as the focal reference.According to Annette Wilke and Oliver Moebus, the diversity of cosmology theories in Hinduism may reflect its tendency to not reject new ideas and empirical observations as they became available, but to adapt and integrate them creatively.The concept of multiverses is mentioned many times in Hindu Puranic literature, such as in the Bhagavata Purana:Every universe is covered by seven layers – earth, water, fire, air, sky, the total energy and false ego – each ten times greater than the previous one. There are innumerable universes besides this one, and although they are unlimitedly large, they move about like atoms in You. Therefore You are called limitless (Bhagavata Purana 6.16.37)Analogies to describe multiple universes also exist in the Puranic literature:Because You are limitless, neither the lords of heaven nor even You(Vishnu ie don't speak for all of us) Yourself can ever reach the end of Your glories.

The countless universes, each enveloped in its shell, are compelled by the wheel of time to wander within You, like particles of dust blowing about in the sky. The śrutis, following their method of eliminating everything separate from the Supreme, become successful by revealing You as their final conclusion (Bhagavata Purana 10.87.41)The layers or elements covering the universes are each ten times thicker than the one before, and all the universes clustered together appear like atoms in a huge combination (Bhagavata Purana 3.11.41)And who will search through the wide infinities of space to count the universes side by side, each containing its Brahma, its Vishnu, its Shiva? Who can count the Indras in them all—those Indras side by side, who reign at once in all the innumerable worlds; those others who passed away before them; or even the Indras who succeed each other in any given line, ascending to godly kingship, one by one, and, one by one, passing away (Brahma Vaivarta Purana)Reincarnation:-

According to Carl Sagan:"The Hindu religion is the only one of the world's great faiths dedicated to the idea that the Cosmos itself undergoes an immense, indeed an infinite, number of deaths and rebirths. It is the only religion in which time scales correspond to those of modern scientific cosmology. Its cycles run from our ordinary day and night to a day and night of Brahma, 8.64 billion years long, longer than the age of the Earth or the Sun and about half the time since the Big Bang."

KUNDALINI AWAKENING-SHIVA AND SHAKTI(Potential energy and Kenetic energy)

One of these poles has a static quality and remains identified with unmanifest consciousness. This quality is called *shiva* and is conceptualized as masculine. Shiva is depicted as being absorbed in the deepest state of meditation—one of formless being, consciousness, and bliss. He remains aloof from and uninterested in manifesting the universe. Shiva has the power to *be*, but not the power to become or act. He is the power holder, but has no energy in his own right. The power that builds the universe arises out of this consciousness.
The other pole is a dynamic, energetic, and creative aspect called shakti—personified as Shakti, the great mother of the universe. From her all form is born. Shakti is the subtlest of created things. She manifests herself as the entire universe: matter, life, and mind.

Shakti is a projection of pure consciousness that veils consciousness with the innumerable illusory manifestations (*maya*) that she brings forth. This is what we call the universe. These two principles—shiva and shakti—are united, but in the world we know an illusion of separation is created between pure consciousness and its manifestations. This leads to confusion and misinterpretation of our world, or mistaking the unreal for the real.

As we know from physics, any activity or force must have a static background. When consciousness manifests itself as the dynamic, creative principle (shakti), she polarizes herself into these two forms. Part of the energy becomes involved in the manifestation itself, while a greater part remains dormant. In Indian mythology, the primal power that remains is symbolized by coiled-up energy—a serpent that supports the universe.

THE CHAKRAS

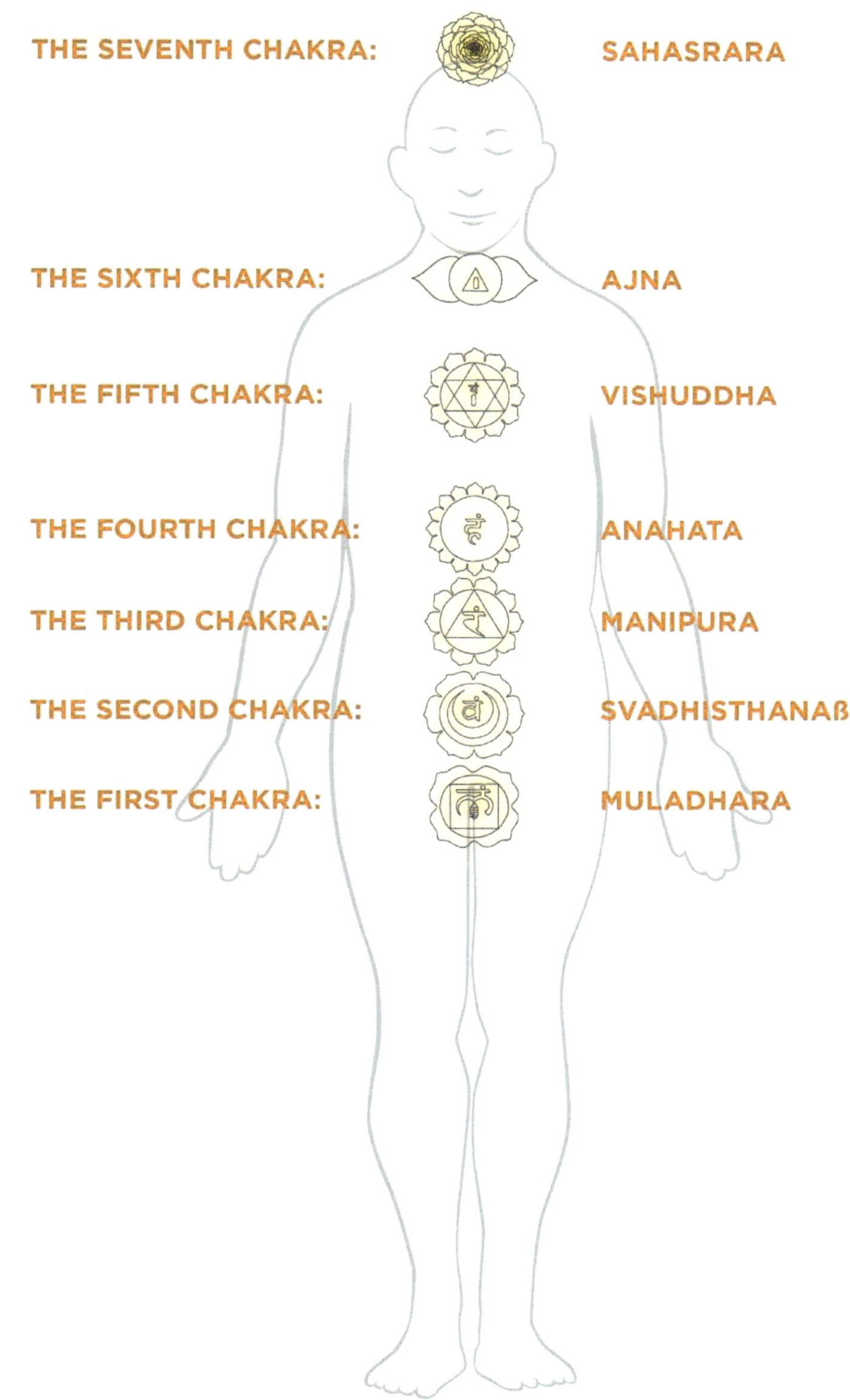

IN SEARCH OF GOD BY GOPALA KRISHNA MERUVA

To genuinely awaken kundalini, preparation is needed. Without long, patient practice in purifying ourselves and strengthening our capacity to assimilate such a flood of energy, the awakening of this power would disturb and confuse us. Even at the physical level such a charge of energy can threaten the body's integrity. This has been metaphorically described in terms of a 10-amp fuse receiving a current of 100 amps. Only after we have developed considerable self-control can this sudden and massive release of awareness be tolerated without danger.

Author's commentary

"The Hindu version of Universe" is guiding principle for modern science in many ways.

History suggest that the modern inventions like Zero, airplane, star birth are taken from Indian philosophical books.

Nostradamus also suggest that after world ends due to wars, Hindu philosophy guides the New World Order.

Now it is evident that the Modern Science ultimately proves what Hindu writings in its Books or Grandhas. According to the calculation presented in Hanuman Chalisa Distance between Sun and Earth = 12000 x 1000 yojanas = 96 million miles = 153.6 million kms, which is much closer to the calculation of the modern scientists.

Tesla's use of ancient Sanskrit terminology in his descriptions of natural phenomena. As early as 1891 Tesla described the universe as a kinetic system filled with energy which could be harnessed at any location. This description of the physical mechanisms of the universe was given before Tesla became familiar with the Vedic science of the eastern Nations of India, Tibet, and Nepal. This science was first popularized in the United States and the west during the three year visit of Swami Vivekananda.

Algebra and the Pythagoras' theorem both originated in India but the credit for these has gone to people from other countries.

Our Ancient scientists discovered the Pythagoras theorem, credit to the Greeks.

'Beejganit' was much before the Arabs, but called Algebra.

Mahabharata says Karna was not born out of his mother's womb. This means people then were aware of genetic science.

There must have been a plastic surgeon who fixed an elephant's head on Ganesha.what the mathematician Aryabhata had said centuries ago, the world has accepted now.

As he witnessed the first detonation of a nuclear weapon on July 16, 1945, a piece of Hindu scripture ran through the mind of Robert Oppenheimer: "Now I am become Death, the destroyer of worlds". It is, perhaps, the most well-known line from the Bhagavad-Gita.

"Yada yada hi dharmasya glanirbhavati bharata |
Abhythanamadharmasya tadatmanam srijamyaham ||

Paritranaya sadhunang vinashay cha dushkritam |
Dharmasangsthapanarthay sambhabami yuge yuge ||

Meaning - I am coming, I am coming, when there is a loss of religion, then I am coming, when the iniquity increases, then I am coming to protect the gentlemen, to destroy the wicked I am coming in to establish religion and I am born in the age of era.

CHAPTER 2
What is the Purpose of Creation

Is the creation had a purpose or an accident.

If God creates this Universe, why so many deaths due to Deceases, Wars, Disasters.

Is "Karma theory" is working or "survival of Fittest theory" working.

Why some people luckiest, memorable, wealthy , innovative ,beautiful, intelligent and skillful.

Is God coming to Earth when "Dharma theory" fails.

Is world stabilizes itself from turbulence or Is turbulence necessary to stabilize the world.

Is a "Computer Programming/God's Code" within DNA of Creatures working. Is the "God's Code" is Local in Brain of Creatures or Non Local like Computer Server or Client. In some people, Is God's Code stimulates them to achieve Greatness. Is this "God's Code" in DNA meant for re start of this Universe on its completion of its cycle.

Is the Earth is a Prison for Creatures which invincible for escape.

If "Reincarnation theory" works, Is it true that humans came from Mars after it is unlivable due to wars. Wars on Earth happened only for Women, Wealth and Land.

The following trends suggest us a step forward to find the intentions of the God/Creator.

<u>Diseases and deaths</u>

1. TuberculosisWorldwide(1800 – 2010).
    There were about 1 billion worldwide from TB in the
    19th and 20th centuries

2. SmallpoxWorldwide   300 million

3. MeaslesWorldwidelast 150 years (as of 2010)
    200 million deaths

4. Second plague pandemic
    including Black Death   100 million deaths approx

5.   MalariaWorldwide (20th century) 250 million deaths

6. Spanish flu Worldwide(1918–1920) 100 million deaths

7. Plague of Justinian(Asia, Europe,Africa(540–590)
     100 million deaths

8.   AIDS pandemicWorldwide(1960–present) (as of 2012)-
     30 million deaths

9.   Third Pandemic of Bubonic Plague
    World- wide(1855–1960)12 million deaths

10. Antonine PlagueRoman Empire(165–180)
    5 million deaths

<u>THE GREATEST natural disasters in recent years</u>

1. 229,000/1975/Typhoon"Nina"—contributed   to
    Banqiao Dam failure China
2. 227,898/2004 Indian Ocean earthquake and
    tsunami/Indian Ocean
3. 145,000/1935 Yangtze river flood,China
4. 143,000/1923 Great Kantō earthquake,Japan
5. 138,866/1991 Bangladesh cyclone Bangladesh

WARS

World War II, 1942-43

Atomic Bomb dropped on Hiroshima and Nagasaki by United States of America

Throughout July 1945 the Japanese mainlands, from the latitude of Tokyo on Honshu northward to the coast of Hokkaido, were bombed just as if an invasion was about to be launched. In fact, something far more sinister was in hand, as the Americans were telling Stalin at Potsdam.

World War II:
total destruction of Hiroshima, Japan

In 1939 physicists in the United States had learned of experiments in Germany demonstrating the possibility of nuclear fission and had understood that the potential energy might be released in an explosive weapon of unprecedented power. On August 2, 1939, Albert Einstein had warned Roosevelt of the danger of Nazi Germany's forestalling other states in the development of an atomic bomb. Eventually, the U.S. Office of Scientific Research and Development was created in June 1941 and given joint responsibility with the war department in the Manhattan Project to develop an atomic bomb.

After four years of intensive and ever-mounting research and development efforts, an atomic device was set off on July 16, 1945, in a desert area near Alamogordo, New Mexico, generating an explosive power equivalent to that of more than 15,000 tons of TNT.

Thus the atomic bomb was born. Truman, the new U.S. president, calculated that this monstrous weapon might be used to defeat Japan in a way less costly of U.S. lives than a conventional invasion of the Japanese homeland. Japan's unsatisfactory response to the Allies' Potsdam Declaration decided the matter. (*See* Sidebar: The decision to use the atomic bomb.) On August 6, 1945, an atomic bomb carried from Tinian Island in the Marianas in a specially equipped B-29 was dropped on Hiroshima, at the southern end of Honshu: the combined heat and blast pulverized everything in the explosion's immediate vicinity, generated fires that burned almost 4.4 square miles completely out, and immediately killed some 70,000 people (the death toll passed 100,000 by the end of the year). A second bomb, dropped on Nagasaki on August 9, killed between 35,000 and 40,000 people, injured a like number, and devastated 1.8 square miles.

<u>World war I</u>

- World War I (WW I), also known as the Great War, lasted from 28 July 1914 to 11 November 1918.

- WW I was fought between the Allied Powers and the Central Powers.

   o The main members of the Allied Powers were France, Russia, and Britain. The United States also fought on the side of the Allies after 1917.

   o The main members of the Central Powers were Germany, Austria-Hungary, the Ottoman Empire, and Bulgaria.

Causes of the War

There was no single event that led to World War I. The war happened because of several different events that took place in the years building up to 1914.

- The new international expansionist policy of Germany: In 1890 the new emperor of Germany, Wilhelm II, began an international policy that sought to turn his country into a world power. Germany was seen as a threat by the other powers and destabilized the international situation.

- Mutual Defense Alliances: Countries throughout Europe made mutual defense agreements. These treaties meant that if one country was attacked, allied countries were bound to defend them.
  o The Triple Alliance-1882 linking Germany with Austria-Hungary and Italy.
  o The Triple Entente, which was made up of Britain, France, and Russia, concluded by 1907.
  o Thus, there were two rival groups in Europe.

- Imperialism: Before World War I, Africa and parts of Asia were points of contention among the European countries because of their raw materials. The increasing competition and desire for greater empires led to an increase in the confrontation that helped push the world into World War I.

- Militarism: As the world entered the 20th century, an arms race had begun. By 1914, Germany had the greatest increase in military buildup. Great Britain and Germany both greatly increased their navies in this time period. This increase in militarism helped push the countries involved into war.

- Nationalism: Much of the origin of the war was based on the desire of the Slavic peoples in Bosnia and Herzegovina to no longer be part of Austria Hungary but instead be part of Serbia. In this way, nationalism led to the War.

- Assassination of Archduke Franz Ferdinand: In June 1914, Archduke Franz Ferdinand, the heir to the throne of Austria-Hungary, was shot while he was visiting Sarajevo in Bosnia. He was killed by a Serbian person, who thought that Serbia should control Bosnia instead of Austria. Because its leader had been shot, Austria-Hungary declared war on Serbia. As a result:
  o Russia got involved as it had an alliance with Serbia.
  o Germany then declared war on Russia because Germany had an alliance with Austria-Hungary.
  o Britain declared war on Germany because of its invasion of neutral Belgium - Britain had agreements to protect both Belgium and France.

- Some of the major battles during the war included the First Battle of the Marne, Battle of the Somme, Battle of Tannenberg, Battle of Gallipoli, and the Battle of Verdun.

Phases of the War

- The conflict developed on several fronts in Europe, Africa, and Asia. The two main scenarios were the Western front, where the Germans confronted Britain, France and, after 1917, the Americans. The second front was the Eastern front in which the Russians fought against Germans and Austro-Hungarians.

- After a brief German advance in 1914, the western front was stabilized and a long and brutal trench warfare started: it was a "war of attrition" (the western front remained immovable). Meanwhile on the Eastern Front the Germans advanced but not decisively.

- In 1917, two events changed the course of the war: the United States joined the Allies and Russia, after the Russian revolution, abandoned the conflict and signed a separate peace.

- Finally after the German offensive in the spring of 1918, the Allied counterattack managed to force a decisive retreat of the German army. The defeat of its Germany's allies and the revolution in Germany that dethroned Wilhem II (German Emperor), brought about the signing of the armistice on November 11, 1918. The Great War was over.

Consequences of the war

- Economic consequences: World War I cost the participating countries a lot of money. Germany and Great Britain spent about 60% of the money their economy produced. Countries had to raise taxes and borrow money from their citizens. They also printed money in order to buy weapons and other things they needed for war. This led to inflation after the war.

- Political Consequences: World War I brought an end to four monarchies: Czar Nicholas II of Russia, Kaiser Wilhelm of Germany, Emperor Charles of Austria and the sultan of the Ottoman Empire had to step down.

  o New countries were created out of old empires. Austria- Hungary was carved up into a number of independent states.

  o Russia and Germany gave land to Poland. Countries in the Middle East were put under the control of Great Britain and France.

  o What was left of Ottoman Empire became Turkey.

- Social Consequences: World war changed society completely. Birth rates declined because millions of young men died (eight million died, millions wounded, maimed, widows and orphans). Civilians lost their land and fled to other countries.

o The role of women also changed. They played a major part in replacing men in factories and offices. Many countries gave women more rights after the war had ended, including the right to vote.

o The upper classes lost their leading role in society. Young middle and lower class men and women demanded a say in forming their country after the war.

- Treaty of Versailles: On June 28, 1919, World War I officially ended with the signing of the Treaty of Versailles. The Treaty of Versailles was an attempt to prevent the world from going into another war.

However, the "war to end all wars" turned out to be the opposite. By ensuring Germany's economic ruin and political humiliation through the Treaty of Versatile, the post-war settlement provided fertile ground for World War II.

<u>The Mahabharata War</u>
<u>[*started on* November 22, 3067 BC]</u>

The *Mahabharata* is an ancient Indian epic where the main story revolves around two branches of a family - the Pandavas and Kauravas - who, in the Kurukshetra War, battle for the throne of Hastinapura. Interwoven into this narrative are several smaller stories about people dead or living, and philosophical discourses. Krishna-Dwaipayan Vyasa, himself a character in the epic, composed it; as, according to tradition, he dictated the verses and Ganesha wrote them down. At 100,000 verses, it is the longest epic poem ever written, generally thought to have been composed in the 4th century BCE or earlier. The events in the epic play out in the Indian subcontinent and surrounding areas. It was first narrated by a student of Vyasa at a snake-sacrifice of the great-grandson of one of the major characters of the story. Including within it the *Bhagavad Gita*, the *Mahabharata* is one of the most important texts of ancient Indian, indeed world, literature.The prelude:
Shantanu, the king of Hastinapur, was married to Ganga (personification of the Ganges) with whom he had a son called Devavrat. Several years later, when Devavrat had grown up to be an accomplished prince, Shantanu fell in love with Satyavati. Her father refused to let her marry the king unless the king promised that Satyavati's son and descendants would inherit the throne. Unwilling to deny Devavrat his rights, Shantanu declined to do so but the prince, on coming to know of the matter, rode over to Satyavati's house, vowed to renounce the throne and to remain celibate throughout his life. The prince then took Satyavati home to the palace so that the king, his father, could marry her. On account of the terrible vow that he'd taken that day, Devavrat came to be known as Bheeshm. Shantanu was so pleased with his son that he granted to Devavrat the boon of choosing the time of his own death.In time, Shantanu and Satyavati had two sons.

Soon thereafter, Shantanu died. Satyavati's sons still being minors, the affairs of the kingdom were managed by Bheeshm and Satyavati. By the time these sons reached adulthood, the elder one had died in a skirmish with some gandharvas (heavenly beings) so the younger son, Vichitravirya, was enthroned. Bheeshm then abducted the three princesses of a neighboring kingdom and brought them over to Hastinapur to be wedded to Vichitravirya. The eldest of these princesses declared that she was in love with someone else, so she was let go; the two other princesses were married to Vichitravirya who died soon afterwards, childless.

Dhritarashtra, Pandu & Vidur;   So that the family line did not die out, Satyavati summoned her son Vyasa to impregnate the two queens. Vyasa had been born to Satyavati of a great sage named Parashar before her marriage to Shantanu. According to the laws of the day, a child born to an unwed mother was taken to be a step-child of the mother's husband; by that token, Vyasa could be considered Shantanu's son and could be used to perpetuate the Kuru clan that ruled Hastinapur. Thus, by the *Niyog* custom, the two queens each had a son of Vyasa: to the elder queen was born a blind son called Dhritarashtra, and to the younger was born an otherwise healthy but extremely pale son called Pandu. To a maid of these queens was born a son of Vyasa called Vidur. Bheeshm brought up these three boys with great care. Dhritarashtra grew up to be the strongest of all princes in the country, Pandu was extremely skilled in warfare and archery, and Vidur knew all the branches of learning, politics, and statesmanship.With the boys grown, it was now time to fill up the empty throne of Hastinapur. Dhritarashtra, the eldest, was bypassed because the laws barred a disabled person from being king. Pandu, instead, was crowned. Bheeshm negotiated Dhritarashtra's marriage with Gandhari, and Pandu's with Kunti and Madri. Pandu expanded the kingdom by conquering the surrounding areas, and brought in considerable war booty. With things running smoothly in the country, and with its coffers full, Pandu asked his elder brother to look after the state affairs, and retired to the forests with his two wives for some time off.

Kauravas & Pandavas; A few years later, Kunti returned to Hastinapur. With her were five little boys, and the bodies of Pandu and Madri. The five boys were the sons of Pandu, born to his two wives through the *Niyog* custom from gods:

the eldest was born of Dharma, the second of Vayu, the third of Indra, and the youngest - twins - of the Ashvins. In the meanwhile, Dhritarashtra and Gandhari too had had children of their own: 100 sons and one daughter. The Kuru elders performed the last rites for Pandu and Madri, and Kunti and the children were welcomed into the palace.Pandavas with Droupadi

All of the 105 princes were subsequently entrusted to the care of a teacher: Kripa at first and, additionally, Drona later. Drona's school at Hastinapur attracted several other boys; Karna, of the Suta clan was one such boy.

It was here that hostilities quickly developed between the sons of Dhritarashtra (collectively called the Kauravas, patronymic of their ancestor Kuru) and the sons of Pandu (collectively called the Pandavas, patronymic of their father).Duryodhana, the eldest Kaurava, tried - and failed - to poison Bheem, the second Pandava. Karna, because of his rivalry in archery with the third Pandava, Arjuna, allied himself with Duryodhan. In time, the princes learnt all they could from their teachers, and the Kuru elders decided to hold a public skills exhibition of the princes.

It was during this exhibition that the citizens became plainly aware of the hostilities between the two branches of the royal family: Duryodhan and Bheem had a mace fight that had to be stopped before things turned ugly, Karna - uninvited as he was not a Kuru prince - challenged Arjuna, was insulted on account of his non-royal birth, and was crowned king of a vassal state on the spot by Duryodhan. It was also around this time that questions began to be raised about Dhritarashtra occupying the throne, since he was supposed to be holding it only in trust for Pandu, the crowned king. To keep peace in the realm, Dhritarashtra declared the eldest Pandava, Yudhishthir, as the crown prince and heir apparent.

The first exile

Yudhishthir's being the crown prince and his rising popularity with the citizens was extremely distasteful to Duryodhan, who saw himself as the rightful heir since his father was the *de facto* king. He plotted to get rid of the Pandavas. This he did by getting his father to send the Pandavas and Kunti off to a nearby town on the pretext of a fair that was held there. The palace in which the Pandavas were to stay in that town was built by an agent of Duryodhan; the palace was made entirely of inflammable materials since the plan was to burn down the palace - together with the Pandavas and Kunti - once they'd settled in. The Pandavas, however, were alerted to this fact by their other uncle, Vidur, and had a counter plan ready; they dug an escape tunnel underneath their chambers. One night, the Pandavas gave out a huge feast which all of the townsfolk came to. At that feast, a forest woman and her five sons found themselves so well-fed and well-drunk that they could no longer walk straight; they passed out on the floor of the hall. That very night, the Pandavas themselves set fire to the palace and escaped through the tunnel. When the flames had died down, the townsfolk discovered the bones of the forest woman and her boys, and mistook them for Kunti and the Pandavas. Duryodhan thought his plan had succeeded and that the world was free of the Pandavas.

Arjuna & Draupadi

Meanwhile, the Pandavas and Kunti went into hiding, moving from one place to another and passing themselves off as a poor brahmin family. They would seek shelter with some villager for a few weeks, the princes would go out daily to beg for food, return in the evenings and hand over the day's earnings to Kunti who would divide the food into two: one half was for the strongman Bheem and the other half was shared by the others. During these wanderings, Bheem killed two demons, married a demoness, and had a demon child called Ghatotkach.

They then heard about a *swayamvar* (a ceremony to choose a suitor) being organized for the princess of Panchal, and went at Panchal to see the festivities. According to their practice, they left their mother home and set out for alms: they reached the *swayamvar* hall where the king was giving away things most lavishly to alms seekers. The brothers sat themselves down in the hall to watch the fun: the princess Draupadi, born of fire, was famed for her beauty and every prince from every country for miles around had come to the *swayamvar*, hoping to win her hand. The conditions of the *swayamvar* were difficult: a long pole on the ground had a circular contraption spinning at its top. On this moving disc was attached a fish. At the bottom of the pole was a shallow urn of water. A person had to look down into this water-mirror, use the bow and five arrows that were provided, and pierce the fish spinning on top. Five attempts were allowed. It was evident that only an extremely skilled archer, such as the now-presumed-dead Arjuna, could pass the test.

Arjuna at the Draupadi Swayamvar

One by one, the kings and princes tried to shoot the fish, and failed. Some could not even lift the bow; some could not string it. The Kauravas and Karna were also present. Karna picked up the bow and strung it in a moment, but was prevented from taking aim when Draupadi declared she would not marry anyone from the Suta clan.

After every one of the royals had failed, Arjuna, the third Pandava, stepped up to the pole, picked up the bow, strung it, affixed all of the five arrows to it, looked down into the water, aimed, shot, and pierced the fish's eye with all of the five arrows in a single attempt. Arjuna had won Draupadi's hand.

The Pandava brothers, still in the guise of poor brahmins, took Draupadi back to the hut they were staying at and shouted for Kunti, "Ma, Ma, come and see what we've brought back today." Kunti, saying, "Whatever it is, share it among yourselves", came out of the hut, saw that it wasn't alms but the most beautiful woman she had ever set her eyes on, and stood stock still as the import of her words sank in on everybody present.

Meanwhile, Draupadi's twin Dhrishtadyumna, unhappy that his royal sister should be married off to a poor commoner, had secretly followed the Pandavas back to their hut. Also following them secretly was a dark prince and his fair brother - Krishna and Balaram of the Yadava clan - who had suspected that the unknown archer could be none other than Arjuna, who had been presumed dead at the palace-burning incident several months ago. These princes were related to the Pandavas - their father was Kunti's brother - but they had never met before. By design or happenstance, Vyasa also arrived at the scene at this point and the Pandava hut was alive for a while with happy cries of meetings and reunions. To keep Kunti's words, it was decided that Draupadi would be the common wife of all of the five Pandavas. Her brother, Dhrishtadyumna, and her father, the king Drupad, were reluctant with this unusual arrangement but were talked around to it by Vyasa and Yudhishthir.

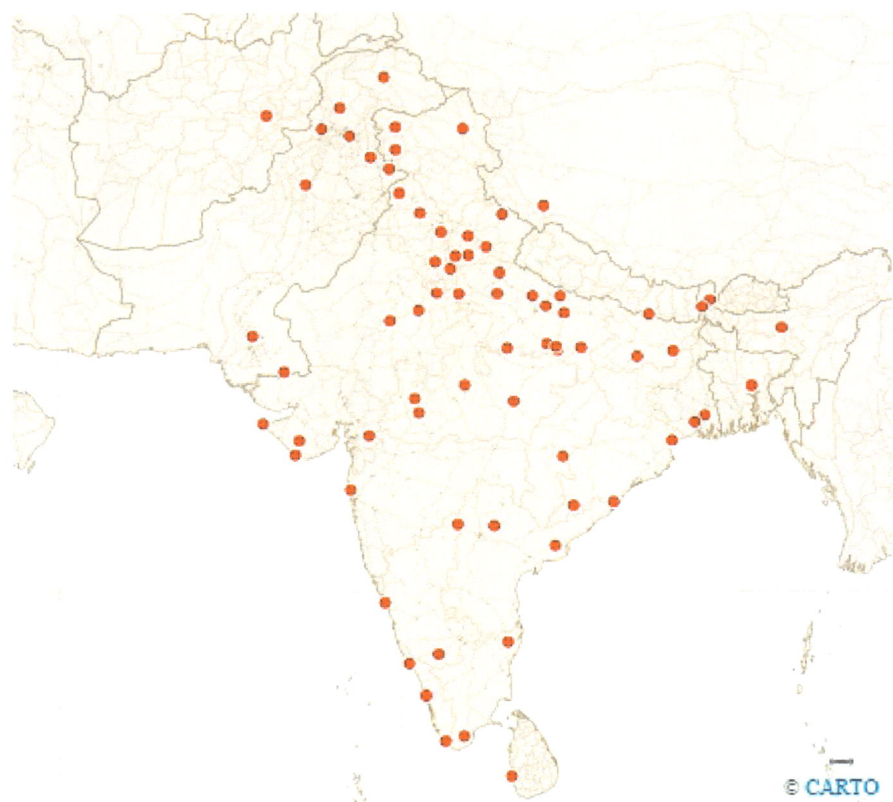

Places in the Mahabharata

Indraprastha & the dice game

After the wedding ceremonies at Panchal were over, the Hastinapur palace invited the Pandavas and their bride back. Dhritarashtra made a great show of happiness on discovering that the Pandavas were alive after all, and he partitioned the kingdom, giving them a huge tract of barren land to settle in and rule over. The Pandavas transformed this land into a paradise. Yudhishthir was crowned there, and he performed a sacrifice that involved all of the kings of the land to accept - either voluntarily or by force - his suzerainty. The new kingdom, Indraprastha, prospered.

Meanwhile, the Pandavas had entered into an agreement among themselves regarding Draupadi: she was to be wife of each Pandava, by turn, for a year. If any Pandava was to enter the room where she was present with her husband-of-that-year, that Pandava was to be exiled for 12 years. It so happened that once Draupadi and Yudhishthir, her husband of that year, were present in the armory when Arjuna entered it to take his bow and arrows. Consequently, he went off in exile during which he toured the entire country, down to its southernmost tip, and married three princesses he met along the way.

The prosperity of Indraprastha and the power of the Pandavas was not something that Duryodhan liked. He invited Yudhisthir to a dice game and got his uncle, Shakuni, to play on his (Duryodhan's) behalf. Shakuni was an accomplished player; Yudhishthir staked - and lost - step by step his entire wealth, his kingdom, his brothers, himself, and Draupadi. Draupadi was dragged into the dice hall and insulted. There was an attempt to disrobe her, and Bheem lost his temper and vowed to kill each and every one of the Kauravas. Things came to such a boil that Dhritarashtra intervened unwillingly, gave the kingdom and their freedom back to the Pandavas and Draupadi, and set them off back to Indraprastha. This angered Duryodhan, who talked his father around, and invited Yudhishthir to another dice game.

This time, the condition was that the loser would go on a 12-year exile followed by a year of life incognito. If they were to be discovered during this incognito period, the loser would have to repeat the 12+1 cycle. The dice game was played. Yudhishthir lost again.

Draupadi Humiliated, Mahabharata

The second exile

For this exile, the Pandavas left their aging mother Kunti behind at Hastinapur, in Vidur's place. They lived in forests, hunted game, and visited holy spots. At around this time, Yudhishthir asked Arjuna to go to the heavens in quest of celestial weapons because, by now, it was apparent that their kingdom would not be returned to them peacefully after the exile and that they would have to fight for it. Arjuna did so, and not only did he learn the techniques of several divine weapons from the gods, he also learnt how to sing and dance from the gandharvas.After 12 years, the Pandavas went incognito for a year.

During this one-year period, they lived in the Virat kingdom. Yudhishthir took up employment as a king's counselor, Bheem worked in the royal kitchens, Arjuna turned himself into a eunuch and taught the palace maidens how to sing and dance, the twins worked at the royal stables, and Draupadi became a handmaiden to the queen. At the end of the incognito period - during which they were not discovered despite Duryodhan's best efforts - the Pandavas revealed themselves. The Virat king was overwhelmed; he offered his daughter in marriage to Arjuna but he declined since he had been her dance teacher the past year and students were akin to children. The princess was married, instead, to Arjuna's son Abhimanyu.At this wedding ceremony, a large number of Pandava allies gathered to draw out a war strategy. Meanwhile, emissaries had been sent to Hastinapur to demand Indraprastha back but the missions had failed. Krishna himself went on a peace mission and failed. Duryodhan refused to give away as much land as was covered by the point of a needle, let alone the five villages proposed by the peace missions. The Kauravas also gathered their allies around them, and even broke away a key Pandava ally - the maternal uncle of the Pandava twins - by trickery. War became inevitable.

Arjuna During the Battle of Kurukshetra

The Kurukshetra war & aftermath

Just before the war bugle was sounded, Arjuna saw arrayed before him his relatives: his great-grandfather Bheeshm who had practically brought him up, his teachers Kripa and Drona, his brothers the Kauravas, and, for a moment, his resolution wavered. Krishna, the warrior *par excellence*, had given up arms for this war and had elected to be Arjuna's charioteer. To him Arjuna said, "Take me back, Krishna. I can't kill these people. They're my father, my brothers, my teachers, my uncles, my sons. What good is a kingdom that's gained at the cost of their lives?" Then followed a philosophical discourse that has today become a separate book on its own - the *Bhagavad Gita*. Krishna explained the impermanence of life to Arjuna, and the importance of doing one's duty and of sticking to the right path. Arjuna picked up his bow again.

सुखदुखे समे कृत्वा लाभालाभौ जयाजयौ। ततो युद्धाय युज्यस्व नैवं पापमंवाप्स्यप्ति।। If you proceed to war treating equally joy and sorrow, gain and loss, victory and defeat, you do not sin. [2.38]कर्मण्येवाधिकारस्ते मा फलेषु कदाचन । मा कर्मफलहेतुर्भूर्मा ते सङ्गोऽस्त्वकर्मणि ॥ You have a right only to work; you have no claim to the fruits thereof. Do not let an expected result dictate your actions; do not sit idle either. [2.47]The battle raged for 18 days. The army totalled 18 *akshauhinis*, 7 on the Panadava side and 11 on the Kaurava (1 *akshauhini* = 21,870 chariots + 21,870 elephants + 65,610 horses + 109,350 soldiers on foot). Casualties on both sides were high. When it all ended, the Pandavas had won the war but lost almost everyone they held dear. Duryodhan and all of the Kauravas had died, as had all of the menfolk of Draupadi's family, including all of her sons by the Pandavas. The now-dead Karna was revealed to be a son of Kunti's from before her marriage to Pandu, and thus, the eldest Pandava and the rightful heir to the throne. The grand old man, Bheeshm, lay dying; their teacher Drona was dead as were several kinsfolk related to them either by blood or by marriage. In about 18 days, the entire country lost almost three generations of its men.
 It was a war not seen on a scale before, it was the Great Indian war, the *Maha-bharat.*After the war, Yudhishthir became king of Hastinapur and Indraprastha. The

Pandavas ruled for 36 years, after which they abdicated in favour of Abhimanyu's son, Parikshit. The Pandavas and Draupadi proceeded on foot to the Himalayas, intending to live out their last days climbing the slopes heavenwards. One by one, they fell on this last journey and their spirits ascended to the heavens. Years later, Parikshit's son succeeded his father as king. He held a big sacrifice, at which this entire story was recited for the first time by a disciple of Vyasa called Vaishampayan.

legacy

Since that time, this story has been retold countless times, expanded upon, and retold again. The *Mahabharata* remains popular to this day in India. It has been adapted and recast in contemporary mode in several films and plays. Children continue to be named after the characters in the epic. The *Bhagvad Gita* is one of the holiest of Hindu scriptures. Beyond India, the *Mahabharata* story is popular in south-east Asia in cultures that were influenced by Hinduism such as Indonesia and Malaysia.

THE HISTORICAL EVIDENCE OF DWARAKA

The discovery of the legendary city of Dwaraka which is said to have been founded by Sri Krishna, is an important landmark in the validation of historical relevance of Mahabharata. It has set at rest the doubts expressed by historians about the historicity of Mahabharata and the very existence of Dvaraka city. It has greatly narrowed the gap of Indian history by establishing the continuity of the Indian civilization from the Vedic age to the present day. The discovery has also shed welcome light on second urbanization in the so-called 'Dark age', on the resuscitation of dharma, on the resumption of maritime trade, and use of Sanskrit language and modified Indus script. Incidentally, scientific data useful for a study of sea level changes and effects of marine environment on metals and wood over long periods has also been generated by underwater exploration.

All this was possible because of the dedicated and daring efforts of marine archaeologists, scientists and technicians of the Marine Archaeology Centre of the National Institute of Oceanography .

The rise in the sea-level in Dwarka is a scientific truth. Studies have proved that the sea considerably and suddenly rose to submerge the city. Harivamsha describes the submerging of Dwarka saying Krishna instructed Arjuna, who was then visiting Dwarka, to evacuate the residents of the city as the sea was going to engulf the city. "On the seventh day (of Krishna saying this), as the last of the citizens were leaving the city, the sea entered the streets of Dwarka."According to experts, there could have been three reasons why the sea entered the land. One, a change in the level of seabed, two, a massive earthquake and three, sudden increase in the level of sea water. Of the three, the last is the most plausible. If it was a change in the level of seabed, some remains of the "tearing off action" on the shore would be visible, which is absent. Earthquake can be ruled out as the structures have not collapsed because of the shake. The third reason is most acceptable as a similar phenomenon had occurred in the shores of Bahrain, around the same time, as some recent findings indicate. It is to be noted here that considerable work has been done on shore and offshore underwater excavations in Bahrain, which has indicated a deep and regular trade and other relations between the western coast and the coasts of the present-day Bahrain region.

<u>WAR BETWEEN RAM AND RAVAN(Ramayan Yudha[5114 BC]</u>

The Yudh Kanda or the War section of the epic Ramayana is replete with details of how Rama and Ravana leading right up to the final arrow that killed Ravana. We crunch that into a short narrative for you here.

Ramayana - that first long epic poem of Bharat told by Rishi (sage) Valmiki in Sanskrit over 24,000 verses - comprises nearly 24,000 verses (mostly set in the Shloka/Anustubh meter). Ramayana is divided into seven Kands

1. Kands:

Bala Kanda,Ayodhya Kanda,Aranya Kanda,Kishkindha Kanda,Sundara Kanda,Yuddha Kanda,Uttara Kanda

2. and about 500 sargas (chapters)

Rama and Ravana fought a fierce battle with bow and arrows for nearly seven days.Ravana's chariot's flag-staff was brought down by Rama's arrows. Every time that Rama cut off Ravana's head, another head would crop up in its place. Soon after that came the fierce and a prolonged chariot-duel between the prince of Ayodhya and the king of Lanka. It was o intense a duel that it shook all the worlds and frightened all people. It is said that when the human-form Lord Rama and demon Ravana engaged in a battle, it was so out of the world that for a while both their respective armies stopped dueling and stood watching the two fight.The Lankan army of demons and Rama's huge army of monkeys fired not an arrow and stood without moving and held on to their weapons but eyes depicting wonder and hearts impressed.Ravana was by no means a pushover. He fought valiantly even as Rama's confidence of victory was overwhelming. Ravana then fired his arrows in the direction of the flagstaff fixed on Rama's chariot. But see the miracle. None of his arrows could reach the Indra's chariot that Rama rode on. All of Ravana's arrows fell to the ground.Rama's arrows, however, tore asunder Ravana's flag-staff that then fell and entered the earth. Absolutely beside himself with rage, Ravana now showered a stream of arrows and also took aim at the horses that pulled Rama's chariot.But those were no ordinary horses, they neither stumbled not stopped. This enraged Ravana further. Now he rained a number of objects in the direction of Rama's chariot.
That included *gadaa* (maces), *hathora* (iron bludgeons), *chakras* (discs), mountains and uprooted trees, axes etc.
When that failed, it was arrows, (*astra*) missiles and magic that he showered next. Ravana tried covering the sky with his missiles. It is said that Ravana saw his impending death, Rama could see victory alone. Now Ravana turned his attention to Matali, Indra's charioteer. But Ravana's attack and arrows could not hurt Matali even a bit.That attack on Matali angered Rama.

As Rama and Ravana battled on, the entire earth, including mountains, groves and forests trembled. The sun too became gloomy and shone less brightly upon Earth and the wind stopped moving.The Gods in Heaven, the Gandharvas and the Kinnaras - all prayed: "May all be well with the cows and Brahmanas, May all the worlds endure forever, May Rama conquer Ravana!"
Vigilant and relentless, Rama chopped off Ravana's head, only to see it grow back. "What is the reason, these arrows by which Mareecha, Khara, Dushana, Kabandha in Kroucha-forest, and Viradha in Dandaka-forest were killed, by which seven Sala trees and the mountains were burst, by which Vali was killed and the ocean shaken up all these arrows which provided immediate succor to me in battle, have proved of little efficacy in the case of Ravana."Finally, Matali, Rama's charioteer suggests that "To kill Ravana you must use the dreaded arrow of Brahma, given to you by Agastya Muni (sage/rishi), which never misses its target". So Rama shot the divine arrow, which had the power of the gods in it. This arrow found its mark and pierced Ravana in the heart, finally killing him.

<u>MODERN EVIDENCE-RAM SETU:</u>An American science channel on Tuesday claimed that the Ram Setu also known as Adam's Bridge and which was claimed to be built by Lord Rama in the Ramayana to rescue his wife Sita from the clutches of Ravana, the evil king of Lanka is a man-made bridge. In a promotional video released on Tuesday by Discovery Communications-owned Science Channel, said that its explorers have found that the bridge located between the landmass of India and Sri Lanka appears to be man-made.

The debate about this structure has been ongoing for some time and the controversy about Setu Samudram Project seems to have been laid to rest now with this new discovery. According to this promotional video Ram Setu is a real man-made bridge that connects India and Sri Lanka. Here are some trivia and mysterious things about the Ram Setu or Adam's Bridge. The promo of the new show 'What on Earth' to be aired on Science Channel offered quite a number of hints to the viewers about the origin of the Ram Setu bridge with quite a few scientists and archaeologists believing it to be man-made.

The video also shows geologist Dr. Alan Lester saying that the rocks of the bridge is 7000-years-old while the sandbar is only 4000-years-old, suggesting that the rocks were brought from elsewhere. Here are some unique and mysterious things about the Ram Setu. Ramayana and Ram Setu Could be True, Claims American Science Channel

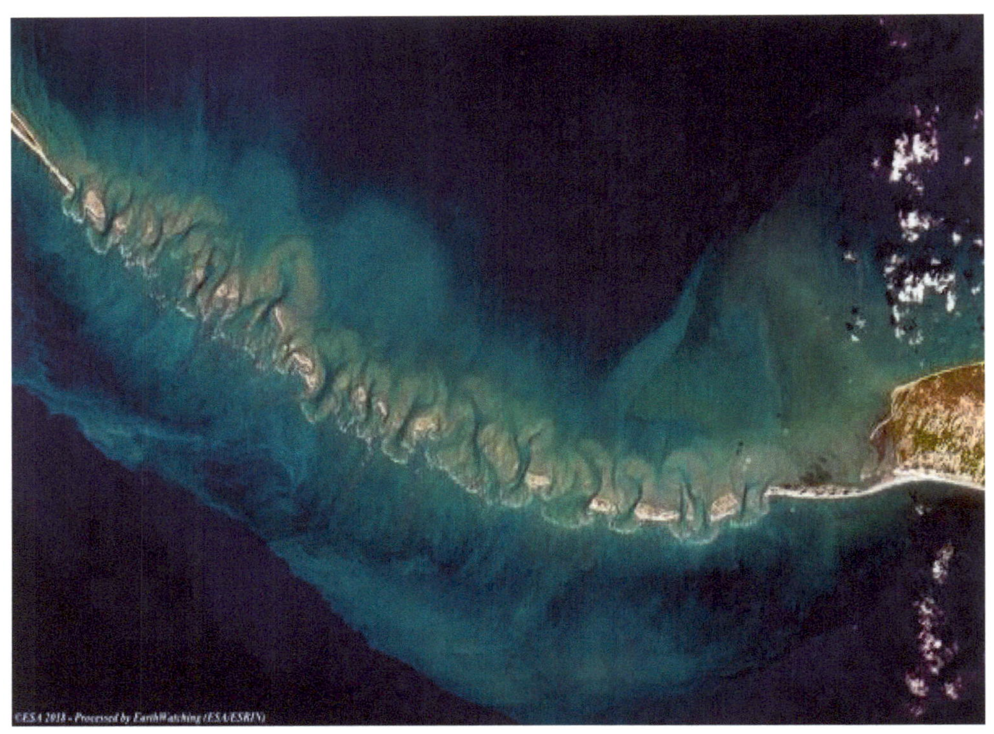

THE GREATEST INVENTIONS THAT CHANGED THE WORLD

1. FIRE – it can be argued that fire was discovered rather than invented. Certainly, early humans observed incidents of fire, but it wasn't until they figured out how to control it and produce it themselves that humans could really make use of everything this new tool had to offer. The earliest use of fire goes back as far as two million years ago, while a widespread way to utilize this technology has been dated to about 125,000 years ago. Fire gave us warmth, protection, and led to a host of other key inventions and skills like cooking. The ability to cook helped us get the nutrients to support our expanding brains, giving us an indisputable advantage over other primates.

2. WHEEL – the wheel was invented by Mesopotamians around 3500 B.C., to be used in the creation of pottery. About 300 years after that, the wheel was put on a chariot and the rest is history. Wheels are ubiquitous in our everyday life, facilitating our transportation and commerce. *Circa 2000 BC, Oxen drawing an ancient Egyptian two-wheeled chariot.*

3. NAIL – The earliest known use of this very simple but super-useful metal fastener dates back to Ancient Egypt, about 3400 B.C. If you are more partial to screws, they've been around since Ancient Greeks (1st or 2nd century B.C.).

4. OPTICAL LENSES – from glasses to microscopes and telescopes, optical lenses have greatly expanded the possibilities of our vision. They have a long history, first developed by ancient Egyptians and Mesopotamians, with key theories of light and vision contributed by Ancient Greeks. Optical lenses were also instrumental components in the creation of media technologies involved in photography, film and television.

5. COMPASS – this navigational device has been a major force in human exploration. The earliest compasses were made of lodestone in China between 300 and 200 B.C. *Circa*

1121 BC, An ancient Chinese magnetic chariot,pointing to the south, moves in accordance with the principle of the magnetic compass.

6. PAPER – invented about 100 BC in China, paper has been indispensable in allowing us to write down and share our ideas.

7. GUNPOWDER – this chemical explosive, invented in China in the 9th century, has been a major factor in military technology (and, by extension, in wars that changed the course of human history).

8. PRINTING PRESS – invented in 1439 by the German Johannes Gutenberg, this device in many ways laid the foundation for our modern age. It allowed ink to be transferred from the movable type to paper in a mechanized way. This revolutionized the spread of knowledge and religion as previously books were generally hand-written (often by monks).

9. ELECTRICITY – utilization of electricity is a process to which a number of bright minds have contributed over thousands of years, going all the way back to Ancient Egypt and Ancient Greece, when Thales of Miletus conducted the earliest research into the phenomenon. The 18th-century American Renaissance man Benjamin Franklin is generally credited with significantly furthering our understanding of electricity, if not its discovery. It's hard to overestimate how important electricity has become to humanity as it runs the majority of our gadgetry and shapes our way of life. The invention of the light bulb, although a separate contribution, attributed to Thomas Edison in 1879, is certainly a major extension of the ability to harness electricity. It has profoundly changed the way we live, work as well as the look and functioning of our cities.

10. STEAM ENGINE – invented between 1763 and 1775 by Scottish inventor James Watt (who built upon the ideas of previous steam engine attempts like the 1712 Newcomen engine), the steam engine powered trains, ships, factories and the Industrial Revolution as a whole.

11. INTERNAL COMBUSTION ENGINE – the 19th-century invention (created by Belgian engineer Etienne Lenoir in 1859 and improved by Germany's Nikolaus Otto in 1876), this engine that converts chemical energy into mechanical energy overtook the steam engine and is used in modern cars and planes. Elon Musk's electric car company Tesla, among others, is currently trying to revolutionize technology in this arena once again.

12. TELEPHONE – although he was not the only one working on this kind of tech, Scottish-born inventor Alexander Graham Bell got the first patent for an electric telephone in 1876. Certainly, this instrument has revolutionized our ability to communicate.

13. VACCINATION – while sometimes controversial, the practice of vaccination is responsible for eradicating diseases and extending the human lifespan. The first vaccine (for smallpox) was developed by Edward Jenner in 1796. A rabies vaccine was developed by the French chemist and biologist Louis Pasteur in 1885, who is credited with making vaccination the major part of medicine that is it today. Pasteur is also responsible for inventing the food safety process of pasteurization, that bears his name.

14. CARS – They were invented in their modern form in the late 19th century by a number of individuals, with special credit going to the German Karl Benz for creating what's considered the first practical motorcar in 1885.

15. AIRPLANE – invented in 1903 by the American Wright brothers, planes brought the world closer together, allowing us to travel quickly over great distances. This technology has broadened minds through enormous cultural exchanges—but it also escalated the reach of the world wars that would soon break out, and the severity of every war thereafter.

16. PENICILLIN – discovered by the Scottish scientist Alexander Fleming in 1928, this drug transformed medicine by its ability to cure infectious bacterial diseases. It began the era of antibiotics.

17. ROCKETS – while the invention of early rockets is credited to the Ancient Chinese, the modern rocket is a 20th century contribution to humanity, responsible for transforming military capabilities and allowing human space exploration.

18. NUCLEAR FISSION – this process of splitting atoms to release a tremendous amount of energy led to the creation of nuclear reactors and atomic bombs. It was the culmination of work by a number of prominent (mostly Nobel Prize-winning) 20th-century scientists, but the specific discovery of nuclear fission is generally credited to the Germans Otto Hahn and Fritz Stassmann, working with the Austrians Lise Meitner and Otto Frisch.

19. SEMICONDUCTORS – they are at the foundation of electronic devices and the modern Digital Age. Mostly made of silicon, semiconductor devices are behind the nickname of "Silicon Valley", home to today's major U.S. computing companies. The first device containing semiconductor material was demonstrated in 1947 by America's John Bardeen, Walter Brattain and William Shockley of Bell Labs.

20. PERSONAL COMPUTER – invented in the 1970s, personal computers greatly expanded human capabilities. While your smartphone is more powerful, one of the earliest PCs was introduced in 1974 by Micro Instrumentation and Telemetry Systems (MITS) via a mail-order computer kit called the *Altair*. From there, companies like Apple, Microsoft, and IBM have redefined personal computing.

21. THE INTERNET – while the worldwide network of computers (which you used to find this article) has been in development since the 1960s, when it took the shape of U.S. Defense Department's ARPANET, the Internet as we know it today is an even more modern invention. 1990s creation of the World Wide Web by England's Tim Berners-Lee is responsible for transforming our communication, commerce, entertainment, politics, you name it

28.

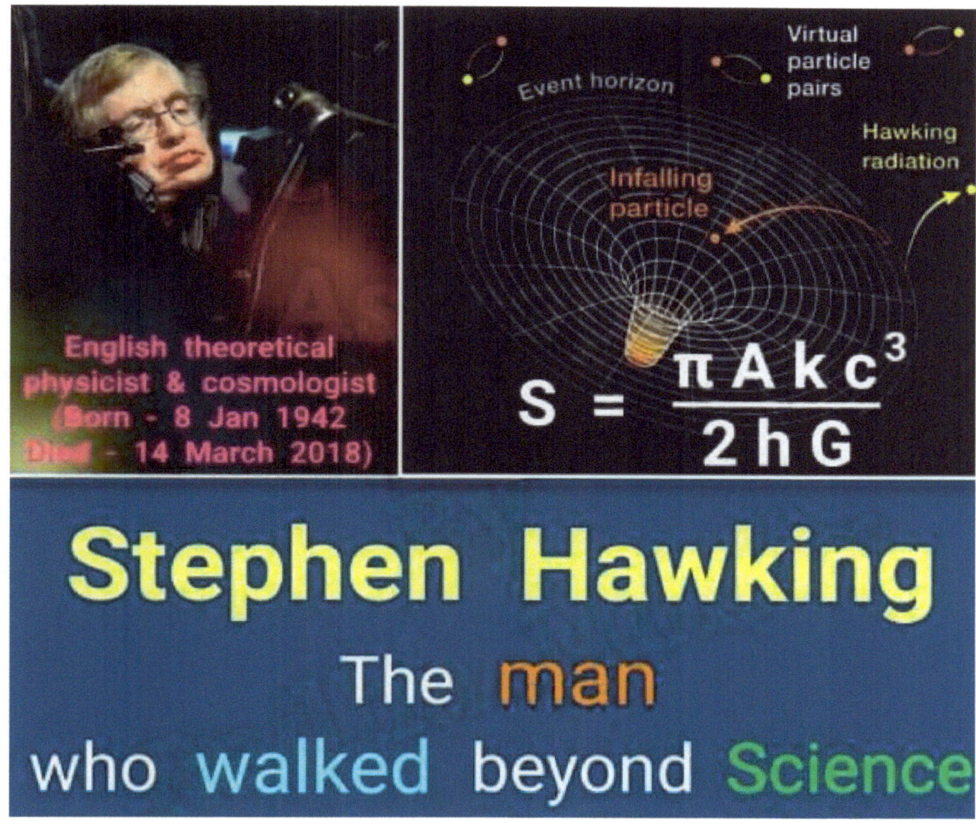

Stephen's Dad was a research biologist while his mom was a medical research secretary. His parent's career must have made Stephen develop a special interest in science from an early age.Just like every other young child, Stephen Hawking was ambitious to reach achieve greater things in life.But in early 1963, Hawking was diagnosed with motor neuron disease. This devastating incident occurred before he celebrated his 21st birthday.With time, the disease began to spread and made Hawking become less mobile. To support Hawking, doctors provided several solutions including the use of wheelchairs.

Despite these challenges, Hawking never lost his focus on science. In 1971, Stephen Hawking proposed a theorem about black hole mechanics.According to Hawking's prediction on Black Hole, "The entire area of a black hole's event horizon in the universe will never decrease."This theorem made Hawking popular across the globe. He also made other predictions in which scientists have proven to be true.Although Steven Hawking died on March 14th, 2018, his scientific contributions will continue to live forever.Today happens to be the posthumous birthday of this great hero. His contributions towards unveiling the universe will never be forgotten in centuries to come.

27.

Narendra Modi is an Indian Politician and the present Prime Minister of India. He is one of the most popular world leaders, and people from other countries like the US also admire and respect him. His ideology and the way of expressing his thoughts in public have a remarkable impact on the people. His speeches and way of handling the government are liked by the people. In this essay on Narendra Modi, students will get to know the life story of Narendra Modi, his early life and his tenure period after becoming the Prime Minister of India.

Early Life of Narendra Modi

Narendra Damodardas Modi was born in Vadnagar on 17th September 1950. Vadnagar is a small village in the Mehsana district of Gujarat. He was the third child among his six siblings. His father, Damodardas Mulchand Modi, was a tea seller and his mother, Hiraba Modi, was a housewife. The entire family lived in a small single-storey house, and they had to struggle to earn their livelihood. In the early years, Narendra Modi helped his father by selling tea at the tea stall, which was set up in the local railway station. As a child, he managed to balance his studies, non-academic life and his contribution to the family tea stall. He was a diligent student and had good debating and reading skills. He loves to read books in the school library and spend hours reading. In childhood, he wanted to serve the nation by joining the Indian Army. But fate had a different plan for him, and later, he entered into the Indian Political System.

Life Story of Narendra Modi

At the age of 17, Narendra Modi left his home and travelled across India. He travelled to various places, including the Himalayas, West Bengal and North East. During his travels, he explored different cultures and traditions of various parts of India. This is the time when he totally lost in spirituality. After travelling for two years, he returned back to home and joined the RSS (Rashtriya Swayamsevak Sangh) in 1972. He worked in it for several years, and his work got recognised by other leaders. Due to his dedication and inclination, he was assigned by the RSS to the BJP in 1985. Later he became a member of the BJP's National Election Committee in 1990, where he got the opportunity to work with other leaders closely.

Narendra Modi served as the Prime minister of India from 2014 to 2019. He was again elected as India's Prime Minister on 30th May 2019 consecutively for the second term. Before becoming the Prime Minister, he was the Chief Minister of Gujarat and served the longest term from October 2001 to May 2014.

Modi is inspired by the motto of 'Sabka Saath, Sabka Vikas, Sabka Vishwas' and aims to build a development-oriented and corruption-free governance. He has a dream and vision for digital India. Initiatives like UPI and Digi locker, which ensure faceless, cashless and paperless Governance, are a few steps towards digital India. With the help of technology, people can easily access education, health care and agriculture services. It will also bring transparency and accountability to the system.Narendra Modi has taken several strong decisions, such as demonetization, surgical strike, repeal of article 370 etc., during his tenure. He has inaugurated the world's largest healthcare programme, Ayushman Bharat. It aims to provide top quality and affordable healthcare to the poor and neo-middle class. He has launched the Pradhan Mantri Jan Dhan Yojana which aims at opening bank accounts for every Indian and making them financially strong. For farmers, the Prime Minister has launched various schemes such as PM Kisan Samman Nidhi and various initiatives for agriculture ranging from Soil Health Cards, E-NAM for better markets and a renewed focus on irrigation.

26.   Nostradamus,   also   called Michel   de Notredame or Nostredame, (born December 14, 1503, Saint-Rémy, France—died July 1/2, 1566, Salon), French astrologer and physician, the most widely read seer of the Renaissance.

Determine whether Nostradamus predicted the French Revolution, rise of Adolf Hitler, and September 11 attacks

Nostradamus began his medical practice in Agen sometime in the 1530s, despite not only never having taken a medical degree but also apparently having been expelled from medical school. In 1544 he moved to Salon, where he gained renown for his innovative medical treatments during outbreaks of the plague at Aix and Lyon in 1546–47. He began making prophecies about 1547, which he published in 1555 in a book entitled *Centuries*. The work consisted of rhymed quatrains grouped in hundreds, each set of 100 called a century. Astrology was then at a peak, and an enlarged second edition, dedicated to the French king, appeared in 1558.ritannica Quiz

Some of his prophecies appeared to be fulfilled, and his fame became so widespread that he was invited to the court of <u>Catherine de Médicis</u>, queen consort of <u>Henry II</u> of <u>France</u>, where he cast the <u>horoscopes</u> of her children. He was appointed physician-in-ordinary by <u>Charles IX</u> in 1564. Nostradamus's prophecies were the subject of many commentaries; contrary to popular belief, however, they were never <u>condemned</u> by the Congregation of the Index, the body set up by the <u>Roman Catholic Church</u> for the examination of books and manuscripts. Because of their cryptic style and content, the prophecies continued to create much controversy. Some of them are thought by believers to have foretold actual historical events that occurred since Nostradamus's time, including certain details of the <u>French Revolution</u> of the 18th century. Others, having no apparent meaning, are said by some to foretell events that have not yet occurred.

25. Napoleon Bonaparte

Napoleon Bonaparte was a French military and political leader who rose to prominence during the French Revolution. Bonaparte was Emperor of the French from 1804 until 1814.He dominated European affairs for nearly two decades while leading France against a series of coalitions.

24. Martin Luther

Martin Luther was a German friar, priest, and professor of theology. He is best known as the seminal figure in the Protestant Reformation. He came to reject several teachings and practices of the Roman Catholic Church. Luther disputed the claim that freedom from God's punishment for sin could be purchased with money.

23. Karl Marx

Karl Marx was a German philosopher, economist, sociologist, journalist, and socialist. His work in economics laid the basis for much of the current understanding of labor and its relation to capital. He has published numerous books during his lifetime.

22. Julius Caesar

Gaius Julias Caesar was a Roman general, statesman, Consul and notable author of Latin prose. Caesar played a critical role in the events that led to the demise of the Roman Republic. Caesar, Crassus, and Pompey formed a political alliance that was to dominate Roman politics for several years.

21. Gautama Buddha

Gautama Buddha, also known as Siddhārtha Gautama or simply 'The Buddha', was a sage on whose teachings Buddism was founded. Buddha lived and taught mostly in eastern India sometime between the sixth and fourth centuries. The name 'Buddha' means "awakened one" or "the enlightened one".

20. Nikola Tesla

Nikola Tesla was a Serbian American electrical engineer, inventor, physicist, and mechanical engineer. Tesla is best known for his contributions to the design of the modern alternating current electricity supply system. He gained experience in telephony and electrical engineering before immigrating to the United States.

19. Adolf Hitler

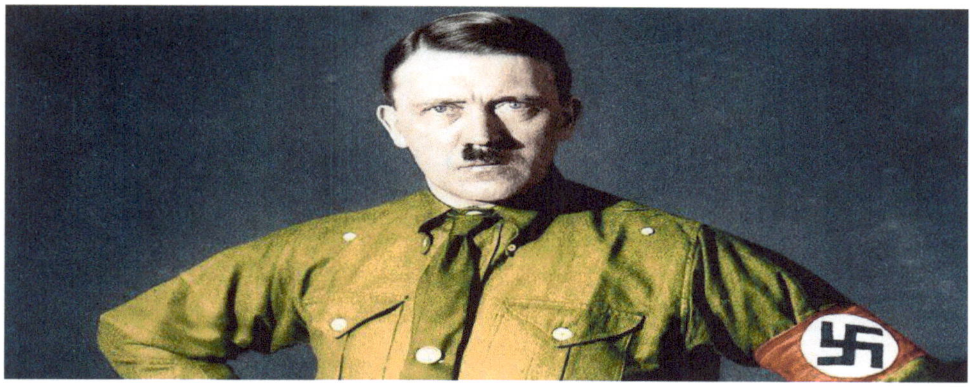

Adolf Hitler was a German politician who was the leader of the Nazi Party. Hitler was Führer of Nazi Germany from 1934 to 1945. Hitler was not only an evil person, but he was also at the center of WWII in Europe. He was manipulating and had control over the German people from 1933 to 1945.

18. Moses

Moses was, according to the Hebrew Bible, a former Egyptian prince later turned prophet, religious leader and lawgiver. The existence of Moses is disputed among archaeologists and Egyptologists, with experts in the field of biblical criticism citing logical inconsistencies.

17. George Washington

George Washington was the first President of the United States. He was also one of the Founding Fathers of the United States and he presided over the convention that drafted the United States Constitution, which replaced the Articles of Confederation.

16. Abraham Lincoln

Abraham Lincoln was the 16th President of the United States. He led the United States and its greatest moral, constitutional and political crisis. Lincoln preserved the Union and strengthened the federal government.

15. Mahatma Gandhi

Mohandas Karamchand Gandhi was the preeminent leader of an Indian independence movement in British-ruled India. He led India into independence and inspired movements for civil rights and freedom across the world. Gandhi has inspired people all over the world to do great.

14. Socrates

Socrates was a Greek philosopher and was one of the founders of Western philosophy. He helped students such as Plato and Xenophon. Plato's dialogues are one of the most comprehensive accounts of Socrates to survive from antiquity.

13. Martin Luther King, Jr.

Martin Luther King, Jr. was an American Baptist minister and activist who was the leader in the Civil Rights Movement. King Jr. is best known for his role in the advancement of civil rights using nonviolent civil disobedience based on his Christian beliefs.

12. William Shakespeare

William Shakespeare was an English poet, playwright, and actor. He is considered to be one of the greatest writers in the English language and the world's pre-eminent dramatist. Shakespeare is often called England's national poet and the "Bard of Avon".

11. Plato

Plato was a philosopher and mathematician. He is considered an essential figure in the development of philosophy. He founded the Academy in Athens, and along with his teacher Socrates and his most famous student, Aristotle, Plato laid the foundation of Western philosophy and science.

10. Charles Darwin

Charles Darwin was an English naturalist and geologist. Darwin is best known for his evolutionary theory. He established that all species of life have descended over time from common ancestors. In a publication with Alfred Russel Wallace, they introduced his scientific theory that this branching pattern of evolution resulted from a process that he called natural selection.

9. Alexander the Great

Alexander the Great was a King of the Ancient Greek kingdom of Macedon and a member of the Argead dynasty. He spent most of his ruling years on an unprecedented military campaign through Asia and Alexander III of Macedon.

8. Galileo Galilei

Galileo Galileo was an Italian mathematician, physicist, engineer, astronomer, and philosopher. His achievements include improvements to the telescope and consequent astronomical observations and support for Copernicanism.

7. Muhammad was the founder of Islam. Believed by Muslims and Bahá'ís to be a prophet and messenger of God. Muhammad is almost universally considered by Muslims as the last prophet sent by God. He was sent to present and confirm the monotheistic teachings preached previously by Adam, Abraham, Moses, Jesus, and other prophets.

6. Aristotle

Aristotle was a Greek philosopher and scientist. He was born in the Macedonian city of Stagira. He remained in the Academy until he turned 37 years old. His writings cover many subjects including biology, logic, ethics, poetry, theater, music and much more.

5. Leonardo Da Vinci

Leonardo di ser Piero da Vinci was an Italian painter, polymath, sculptor, musician, mathematician, inventor, engineer, and botanist. Da Vinci is considered to be one of the greatest painters in history. He is a true genius, and he has often been described as the archetype of the Renaissance Man.

4. Isaac Newton

Sir Isaac Newton was an English physicist and mathematician. Newton is best known for being one of the most influential scientists of all time and as a key figure in the scientific revolution.

3. Albert Einstein

Albert Einstein was a German-born physicist. His work is also known for its influence on the philosophy of science. Einstein received the 1921 Nobel prize in Physics for his "services to theoretical physics". He is considered to be one of the most influential people in the world.

2. Jesus Christ

Jesus is also referred to as Jesus of Nazareth is the central figure of Christianity. Christianity regards Jesus as the awaited Messiah of the Old Testament and refers to him as Jesus Christ. Jesus is the most influential person in the world.

Krishna, Sanskrit Kṛṣṇa, one of the most widely revered and most popular of all Indian divinities, worshipped as the eighth incarnation (avatar, or *avatara*) of the Hindu god Vishnu and also as a supreme god in his own right. Krishna became the focus of numerous *bhakti* (devotional) cults, which have over the centuries produced a wealth of religious poetry, music, and painting. The basic sources of Krishna's mythology are the epic *Mahabharata* and its 5th-century-CE appendix, the *Harivamsha*, and the Puranas, particularly Books X and XI of the *Bhagavata-purana*. They relate how Krishna (literally "black," or "dark as a cloud") was born into the Yadava clan, the son of Vasudeva and Devaki, who was the sister of Kamsa, the wicked king of Mathura (in modern Uttar Pradesh). Kamsa, hearing a prophecy that he would be destroyed by Devaki's child, tried to slay her children, but Krishna was smuggled across the Yamuna River to Gokula (or Vraja, modern Gokul), where he was raised by the leader of the cowherds, Nanda, and his wife Yashoda.The child Krishna was adored for his mischievous pranks; he also performed many miracles and slew demons.

As a youth, the cowherd Krishna became renowned as a lover, the sound of his flute prompting the _gopi_s (wives and daughters of the cowherds) to leave their homes to dance ecstatically with him in the moonlight. His favourite among them was the beautiful Radha. At length, Krishna and his brother Balarama returned to Mathura to slay the wicked Kamsa. Afterward, finding the kingdom unsafe, Krishna led the Yadavas to the western coast of Kathiawar and established his court at Dvaraka (modern Dwarka, Gujarat). He married the princess Rukmini and took other wives as well.

World Religions & Traditions

Krishna refused to bear arms in the great war between the Kauravas (sons of Dhritarashtra, the descendant of Kuru) and the Pandavas (sons of Pandu), but he offered a choice of his personal attendance to one side and the loan of his army to the other. The Pandavas chose the former, and Krishna thus served as charioteer for Arjuna, one of the Pandava brothers. On his return to Dvaraka, a brawl broke out one day among the Yadava chiefs in which Krishna's brother and son were slain. As the god sat in the forest lamenting, a huntsman, mistaking him for a deer, shot him in his one vulnerable spot, the heel, killing him.Krishna's personality is clearly a composite one, though the different elements are not easily separated. Vasudeva-Krishna was deified by the 5th century BCE. The cowherd Krishna was probably the god of a pastoral community. The Krishna who emerged from the blending of these figures was ultimately identified with the supreme god Vishnu-Narayana and, hence, considered his avatar. His worship preserved distinctive traits, chief among them an exploration of the analogies between divine love and human love. Thus, Krishna's youthful dalliances with the _gopi_s are interpreted as symbolic of the loving interplay between God and the human soul.

Krishna and the flute: The rich variety of legends associated with Krishna's life led to an abundance of representation in painting and sculpture. The child Krishna (Balakrishna) is depicted crawling on his hands and knees or dancing with joy, a ball of butter held in his hands.

The divine lover—the most common representation—is shown playing the flute, surrounded by adoring *gopi*s. In 17th- and 18th-century Rajasthani and <u>Pahari painting</u>, Krishna is characteristically depicted with blue-black skin, wearing a yellow <u>dhoti</u> (loincloth) and a crown of peacock feathers.

TOP SPORT PERSON IN THE WORLD

Ranking	Sportsperson	Sport
1	Cristiano Ronaldo	Football
2	Lebron James	Basketball
3	Neymar	Football
4	Michael Jordan	Basketball
5	Tom Brady	American Football
6	Conor McGregor	MMA
7	Mike Tyson	Boxing
8	Lionel Messi	Football
9	Virat Kohli	Cricket
10	Tyson Fury	Boxing

According to a study by renowned cosmetic surgeon Julian De Silva, <u>Bella Hadid</u> holds the crown for the most beautiful woman in the world. De Silva compiled his list of top <u>10</u> women by using what is referred to as the Golden Ratio theory. This "divine proportion" was theorized in Ancient Greece, then used during the Renaissance by esteemed <u>artists</u> to create perfect works of art. Relishing in modern-day time, the <u>cosmetic</u> surgeon made completely different use of the rule in order to reveal which women are mathematically close to physical perfection.In order to calculate this golden number of beauty, De Silva based his list on a calculated measurement of the size and position of the eyes, eyebrows, nose, <u>lips</u>, chin and jaw. Among all the data collected, Bella Hadid ranked highest with a result of 94.35% of symmetry. While keeping in mind that beauty is celebrated in all forms of imperfection, De Silva's list is taken in stride when considering the societal standards of cosmetic beauty. 1. Bella Hadid (94.35%)

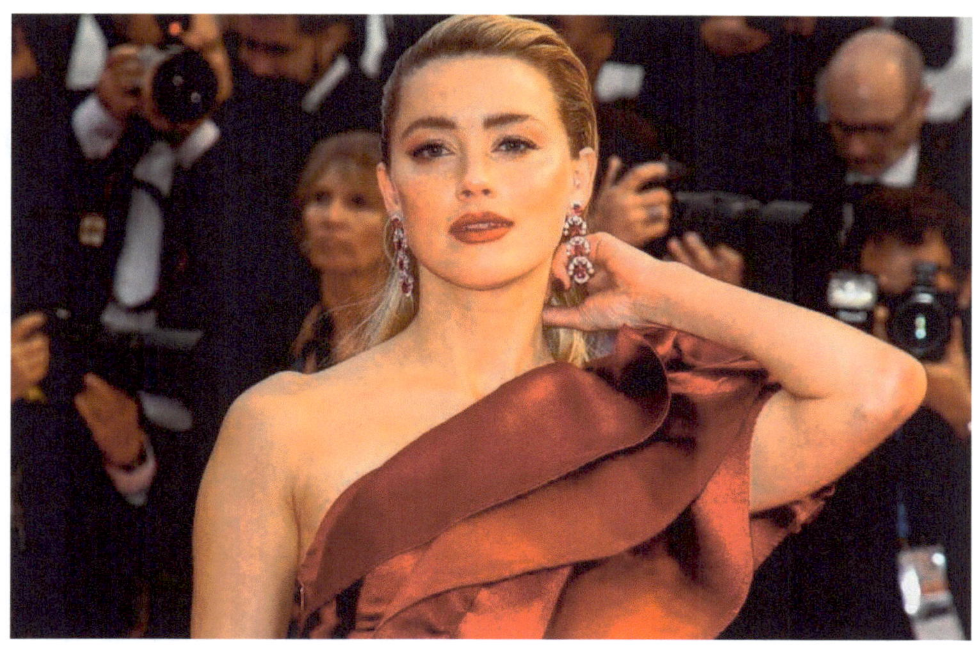

IN SEARCH OF GOD BY GOPALA KRISHNA MERUVA

Top 5 Most Popular Actors in the World 2022

Bruce le

Born: November 27, 1940
San Francisco, California
Died: July 20, 1973
Hong Kong
American actor and martial arts master

Actor and martial arts expert Bruce Lee combined the Chinese fighting art of kung fu with the grace of a ballet dancer. He helped make kung fu films a new art form before his sudden and mysterious death in 1973.

The "strong one"

In 1939 Lee Hoi Chuen, a Chinese opera singer, brought his wife Grace and three children from Hong Kong to San Francisco, California, while he performed in the United States. On November 27, 1940, the Lees had another son. His mother called the boy Bruce because the name meant "strong one" in Gaelic. His first film appearance, at the age of three months, was in *Golden Gate Girl* (1941). Although Hong Kong was occupied by Japanese troops, the Lees then decided to return home, where Lee's film appearances continued, numbering around twenty by the time he graduated from high school.As a teenager Lee was both a dancer, winning a cha-cha championship, and a gang member, risking death on the Hong Kong streets. To improve his fighting skills, he studied the Chinese martial arts of kung fu. He absorbed the style called wing chun, which was developed by a woman named Yim Wing Chun, and he began adding his own improvements. Lee's film career continued, and he was offered a large contract. But when he got into trouble with the police for fighting, his mother sent him to the United States to live with friends of the family.

Teacher and actor

After finishing high school in Edison, Washington, Lee enrolled at the University of Washington, supporting himself by giving dance lessons and waiting tables.

While teaching kung fu to fellow students, he met Linda Emery, whom he married in 1964. Lee developed a new fighting style called jeet kune do and opened three schools on the West Coast to teach it. He also landed a part in the television series *The Green Hornet* as Kato, the Hornet's assistant. Kato used a dramatic fighting style quite unlike that which Lee taught in his schools. The show was cancelled after one season, but fans would long remember Lee's role.

Lee went on to appear on shows such as *Longstreet* and *Ironside* and in the film *Marlowe* (1969), playing a high-kicking villain. Unhappy with the number and quality of roles available to Asian Americans in Hollywood, Lee and his family, including son Brandon and daughter Shannon, moved back to Hong Kong in 1971. Lee soon released the movie known to U.S. audiences as *Fists of Fury.* The story, featuring Lee as a fighter seeking revenge on those who had killed his kung fu master, was not very original, but with his graceful movements, his good looks and charm, and his acting ability, Lee was a star in the making.

Sudden death

Fists of Fury set box-office records in Hong Kong that were broken only by Lee's next film, *The Chinese Connection* (1972). Lee established his own film company, Concord Pictures, and began directing movies. The first of these would appear in the United States as *Way of the Dragon.* Lee was excited about his future. He told a journalist, "I hope to make ... the kind of movie where you can just watch the surface story, if you like, or can look deeper into it." Unfortunately, on July 20, 1973, three weeks before his fourth film, *Enter the Dragon,* was released in the United States, Lee died suddenly.

The official cause of Lee's death was brain swelling as a reaction to aspirin he had taken for a back injury. But there were rumors that he had been poisoned by either the Chinese mafia or powerful members of the Hong Kong film industry. Others said that Lee's purchase of a house in Hong Kong had angered neighborhood demons, who then placed a curse on him to last for three generations.

This theory was revived on June 18, 1993, when Lee's son Brandon also died under strange circumstances. While filming the movie *The Crow,* he was shot by a gun that was supposed to contain only blanks (which produce the appearance of a gunshot but cause no bullet to be fired) but in fact had a live round in its chamber.

Bruce Lee.

Bruce Lee's movies, though few in number, created a new art form. By the 1990s *Enter the Dragon* alone had earned more than $100 million, and Lee's influence could be found in the work of many Hollywood action heroes such as Jean-Claude Van Damme, Steven Seagal, and Jackie Chan. In 1993 Jason Scott Lee (no relation) appeared in *Dragon: The Bruce Lee Story.*

2.Jackie Chan

Chan Kong-sang SBS MBE PMW who is worldwide popular as Jackie Chan is one of the most popular actors in the world from China. This legendary actor was born on 7th April 1954 in Victoria Peak, Hong Kong. He is a multi-talented person who knows excellent martial art, action choreography, screenwriting, and singing.

Jackie Chan made famous martial art and stunts worldwide through his movies. He is popular among people as an action hero and best martial artist who do all stunt scenes himself. He knows Chinese martial arts Kung Fu and Hapkido.

Jackie Chan is doing movies since 1960 and has done more than 150 movies so far. Some of his popular movies are Armour of God 2, Wheels on Meals, Drunken Master, Police Story, and many more. Currently, he is perceived as the most recognized star in the world and among the highest-paid actors in the world.

3.Will Smith

American actor will smith is another world's most popular actor in 2022. Smith was born on 25th September 1968 and started her acting career with the television series "The Fresh Prince of Bel-Air". Then he got the chance to act on several blockbuster movies like Muhammad Ali and The pursuit of happiness. Currently, he is one of the most successful Hollywood actors.Will Smith has achieved a lot of awards for his exceptional acting talent. Till now he has been nominated for 5 times Golden Globe awards and two academic awards. He has a record of winning 4 Grammy awards also for his best acting performances.

People who have the Highest IQ in the World

1. Rick Rosner: IQ 192–198

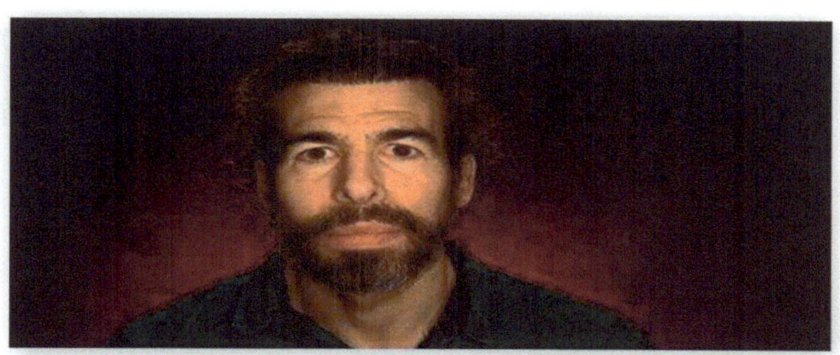

Rick Rosner has taken over 30 IQ tests, demonstrating his IQ is between 192 and 198, depending on how the tests determine their scores. Before the allegedly second-smartest man in the world became a TV writer, he served as a bouncer, stripper, and nude model. He famously sued the ABC network for a false question after losing *Who Wants to Be a Millionaire?* At the $16,000 level, but lost the case.

2. Evangelos Katsioulis: IQ 198

With a score of 198, Evangelos Katsioulis, MD, MSc, MA, Ph.D., has the highest IQ in the world as per World Genius Directory. This Greek psychiatrist holds degrees in medical research technology and philosophy.

3. Nathan Leopold: IQ 200

The notorious Nathan Leopold had an IQ of 200 and spoke 9 languages by age 18, but he didn't utilize his intelligence for the greater good. When he was 19, he was arrested for murder in 1924 after attempting to commit the "perfect crime"—the kind of crime that never gets solved. Leopold spent 33 years in jail before getting released on parole. He died in 1971.

4. Ainan Cawley: IQ 263

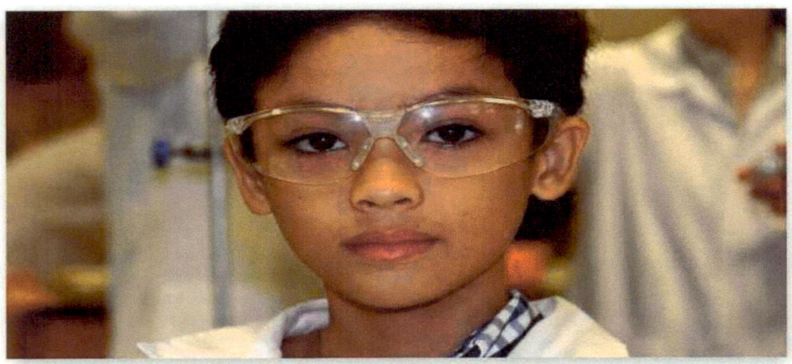

This former Irish child genius, who's now 21, has an IQ of 263. At 8 years old, he was already taking third-year chemistry courses at Singapore Polytechnic, and by the time he was 9, he'd learned the first 518 decimal places of pi. He also seems to have a knack for entertainment, having penned the script and composed music for a short film, Reflection, at age 12.

5. Johann Goethe: IQ 210–225

When American electrochemical engineer Libb Thims set out to discover the person with the highest IQ in history, he used a methodology that indicates their IQ based on how much they achieved every 10 years. This came in handy when trying to rank people who predated IQ tests. Based on his approach, it was calculated that German Renaissance man Johann Goethe was the person with the highest IQ of all time, with a score ranging from 210 to 225. While generally labeled a philosopher, Goethe was also an accomplished scientist and poet.

6. Sho Yano: IQ 200

American physician Sho Yano began college at age nine and earned an MD and Ph.D. by age 21. He began composing music when he was 4, but he's put his emphasis on child neurology.

7. Christopher Langan: IQ 174–210

Usually referred to as "the smartest man in America," Christopher Langan is a former cowboy, current horse rancher, and a self-reliant researcher and reality theorist. One of his best pieces is his Cognitive-Theoretic Model of the Universe, which he refers to as "the CTMU" and pronounced as *cat-mew.* In an interview with *Esquire in 2007*, Langan said that it was "a true 'Theory of Everything,' a cross between John Archibald Wheeler's 'Participatory Universe' and Stephen Hawking's 'Imaginary Time' theory of cosmology." He is among the people with the highest IQ in the world.

8. Jacob Barnett: IQ 170

At two years old, Jacob Barnett was diagnosed with moderate to severe autism, and doctors implied he'd never learn to tie his own shoes. He's learned that task. The American child prodigy completed grades 6 through 12 in less than a year, then moved to college at age 10. He was a published physicist when he was 13. Now he's 21 and working toward his Ph.D.

9. Marnen Laibow-Koser: IQ 268

When Marnen Laibow-Koser was tested as a kid, he was given a projected IQ of 268. Now, he's a songwriter and musician living in Randolph, Massachusetts. He has been both playing and composing music since the age of 3.

10. Adragon De Mello: IQ 400

In 1988, when Adragon De Mello graduated from the University of California with a degree in computational mathematics at the age of 11. At that time, he was the youngest college graduate in the United States. Though he was said to have a projected IQ of 400, De Mello hasn't been in the public eye much in the past 20 years. In 2001 when he was a 24-year-old "high-tech worker," he took his father's custody, who was dying of bladder cancer.

11. Leonardo da Vinci: IQ 180–220

While IQ tests weren't available when Leonardo da Vinci was, it is now calculated that his score would have been between 180 and 220. This makes sense when you consider it: With skills ranging from art and science to music and architecture, da Vinci didn't just work in diverse fields—he excelled at them. He was so ahead of his time that numerous inventions (like flying machines, the telescope, and the submarine) didn't come to fruition until long after his death.

12. Isaac Newton: IQ 190–200

Sir Isaac Newton is a physicist—far ahead of his time. Though he's best recognized for his universal principles of gravity, the 17th-century philosopher was also a mathematician, astronomer, and writer. His IQ score would fall between 190 and 200, depending on the criteria used.

The 5 Richest People in the World

5. <u>Bernard Arnault</u> Net Worth $70 Billion

Bernard Arnault is a French businessman and current CEO of luxury goods conglomerate LVMH, which is made up of companies such as Louis Vuitton, Moet & Chandon, and Fendi. He got his start in business after college, when he joined his father's company, before eventually heading his own company selling luxury condominiums in Miami, Florida. After returning home to France, he became CEO of fashion brand Christian Dior, which his family holds a 73% stake in. Christian Dior in turn is a 41% owner in LVMH, and the Arnault family also have a 5.7% direct stake in LVMH as well.

4. <u>Vladimir Putin</u> Net Worth $70 Billion

Vladimir Putin is a Russian politician, currently serving his second term as the President of Russia. His first Presidential term lasted from 2000 – 2008, and he has also served as Prime Minister of Russia from 1999 – 2000, and 2008 – 2012.

3. <u>Warren Buffett</u> Net Worth $75 Billion

Warren Buffett is an American entrepreneur, widely consid- ered to be the greatest investor of all time. He is also the CEO of Berkshire Hathaway, a multinational conglomerate holding company that owns GEICO, Dairy Queen, and Duracell, as well as holdings in companies such as American Express, Apple, and several major US airline carriers. Despite his immense success, Buffett is also known to be incredibly humble. He still lives in Omaha, Nebraska, in a modest house he bought in 1956.

He also has pledged to give away 99% of his net worth to charity before he dies as part of The Giving Pledge, with 83% of the money to go to the Bill and Melinda Gates Foundation.As of this writing, Warren Buffett's net worth is $75 billion. He is 89 years old. That makes him the oldest billionaire on this list.

2. <u>Bill Gates</u> Net Worth $102 Billion

Bill Gates is an American business magnate, philanthropist, author. He is also the co-founder and former CEO of software company Microsoft, which has become the largest PC software company in the world since its beginnings in 1975. Today, Gates actually owns less than 1.3% of Microsoft; he has sold most of his shares over the years to fund Cascade Investment LLC, a vehicle he uses to invest in hundreds of other companies. In 2010, he pledged with his wife Melinda Gates as part of The Giving Pledge, to donate at least half of their wealth over the course of time, to charity. The couple now operate the Bill & Melinda Gates Foundation, the largest transparent charitable foundation in the world.

1. <u>Jeff Bezos</u> Net Worth $111 Billion

Jeff Bezos is an American philanthropist, businessman and investor who is best known for being the founder and CEO of Amazon. What originally started as a simple online bookstore, Amazon has since expanded into a massive global retailer and household name. After his divorce in 2019, his ex-wife MacKenzie Bezos received 19.7 million shares as part of their divorce settlement, valued at $36 billion at the time. Despite his success, Bezos is not the "Richest Person of All Time" when adjusting for inflation. He has yet to catch up to figures such as oil tycoon John D. Rockefeller, who was worth an inflation- adjusted $340 billion when he died.As of this writing, March 15, 2020, Jeff Bezos' net worth is $111 billion which makes him the #1 richest person in the world.

5 of the luckiest people in human history

1.<u>Adolphe Sax</u>;

The saxophone is one of the most recognizable musical instruments in the world, both in appearance and sound. However, the horn may have never come into being if its inventor, <u>Adolphe Sax</u>, hadn't survived a logic-defying 7 incredibly close calls with death as a child before he even reached the age of 10.A native of Belgium, Sax was born in 1814 and became a musician (he played the clarinet and the flute) and inventor (he developed several other instruments). His affinity from music and innovation seems to have come from his father, who was a carpenter and produced musical instruments by order of the King. It was under his father's direction that a young Sax performed such incredible feats as carving a clarinet and two flutes completely out of ivory.; something that had been previously thought to be impossible.Having grown up immersed in music, Sax pursued it profes- sionally as he got older. Moving to France, he decided to produce a new range of instruments for the French military, which was still large and resplendent even after the departure of Napoleon. One of these new-aged military instruments he worked on was developing what became known as the saxophone, for which he filed for a patent in 1846. It exploded in popularity over the years, although not so much for its original intended military use. There are currently an estimated 300,000 professional sax players in the world and approximately 27,000 new instruments are produced in the United States annually.Sax had a seeming affinity for brushes with death throughout his life. Even as an adult, he suffered for years with lip cancer before making a recovery and living to the age of 79, passing away in 1894.

However, it was his experiences as a child that were very unusual and left many to wonder how he managed to survive to not only invent his eponymous instrument but also to live to such a respectable age.It's still a mystery as to what made Sax so prone to incredibly bizarre close calls as a child, but they piled up before he reached adolescence. These included:He mistook a bowl of diluted sulfuric acid to be milk and drank it.His father's work exposed him to different chemicals and he suffered poisoning from acute exposure to varnish on three separate occasions when freshly stained furniture was left to dry overnight in the room in which he slept.On separate occasions he accidentally swallowed a needle and also fell out of a third-story window and hit his head on a paving stone on the ground. Differing accounts from his fall indicate that he was either laid up for a week or possibly even in a coma for that same period of time.Of course, there were also the incidents when he was seriously burned when he was near exploding gunpowder that knocked him across his father's workshop, and another time when he stumbled on to a hot cast-iron stove and had burns all over his torso.Finally, on another occasion, Sax was hit in the head by a slate tile that slid off a roof and he fell into an adjacent river, nearly drowning in the process.Sax's childhood neighbors called him ,"Little Sax, the ghost." His own mother is reported to have once said of her death- defying son, "He's a child condemned to misfortune; he won't live." Miraculously, he did live, surviving calamity after calamity on his way to making a significant mark on the world and living to a ripe old age.

2. <u>Lena Påhlsson</u> found a wedding ring that disappeared 16 years ago while harvesting vegetables in her garden. A carrot grew through the ring, and the ring came up with the vegetable.

3. <u>Steve</u> grew up without his mother and has been looking for her for years. As it turns out, he was searching for the wrong last name. A coincidence helped him find his mom. Steve began to work in a big chain store and told his boss about his struggle.The boss recognized Steve's mom's last name. So it happens, she was working at a different store of this chain.

4.<u>Virginia</u> always chose the same digit combination for her lottery tickets. The first number stood for the number of years for which her parents have been married, and the second their age at the year of their wedding. In 2012, she signed 2 tickets with the same numbers by accident, each of which brought her a million dollars.

5.<u>Tsutomu Yamaguchi</u> is the only person who survived in the two of the nuclear attacks on Japan. He was on a business trip in Hiroshima when the nuclear attack happened, only 3 kilometers away from the explosion. He was seriously burned but ok. Three days later, he returned to his workplace in Nagasaki, where the second explosion happened.

CHAPTER 3

The Western Model of this Universe

Remarkable Theories/discoveries

1.   Pythagorean theorem, the well-known geometric theorem that the sum of the squares on the legs of a right triangle is equal to the square on the hypotenuse (the side opposite the right angle)—or, in familiar algebraic notation, $a^2 + b^2 = c^2$

2.   Einstein theory: energy (E) equals mass (m) times the speed of light (c) squared (^{2}), or $E=mc^2$. The secret the equation revealed—that mass and energy are different forms of the same thing.

3.   Pi is a never-ending number:It can't be expressed as a fraction; it doesn't end with a repeating pattern (like the decimal expression of 1/3, 0.33333..., in which the threes repeat forever), or terminate after a certain number of decimal places (like 3/4, or . 75). It just keeps going, going, and going.

4.   jellyfish Turritopsis dohrnii. These small, transparent animals hang out in oceans around the world and can turn back time by reverting to an earlier stage of their life cycle

5.   The human eye can only see between 430-770 THz.Our ears can only detect sound between 20Hz -20KHz. These ranges make up a fraction of the total sound and light frequency range.This means there is lot that we cannot see or hear

A new report in 2014 confirms the Milky Way as a member of the Laniakea Supercluster. The Caelum Supercluster is a collection of over 550,000 galaxies. **It is the largest of all galaxy superclusters.**

five elements

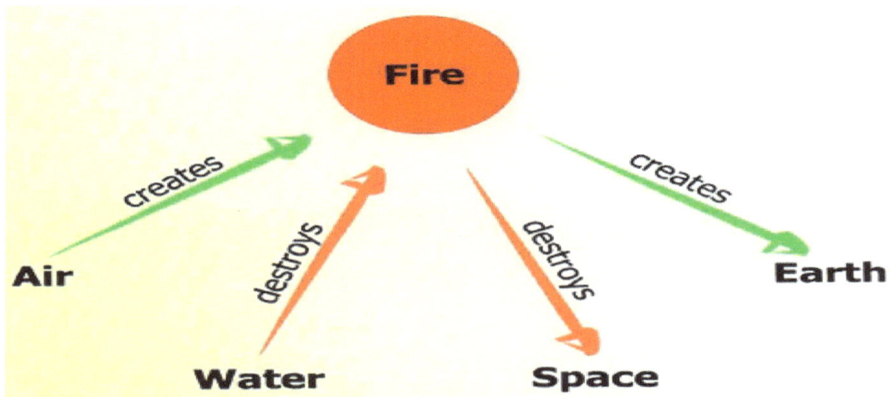

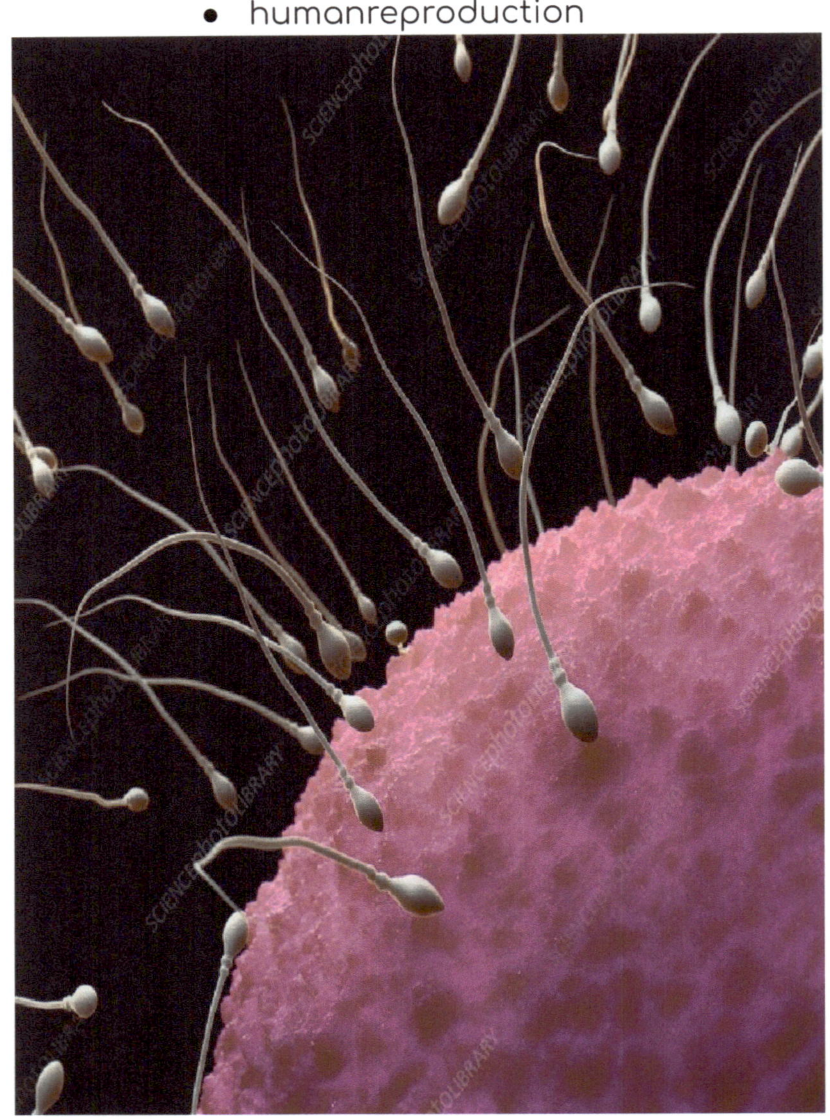

IN SEARCH OF GOD BY GOPALA KRISHNA MERUVA

Universe Image

IN SEARCH OF GOD BY GOPALA KRISHNA MERUVA

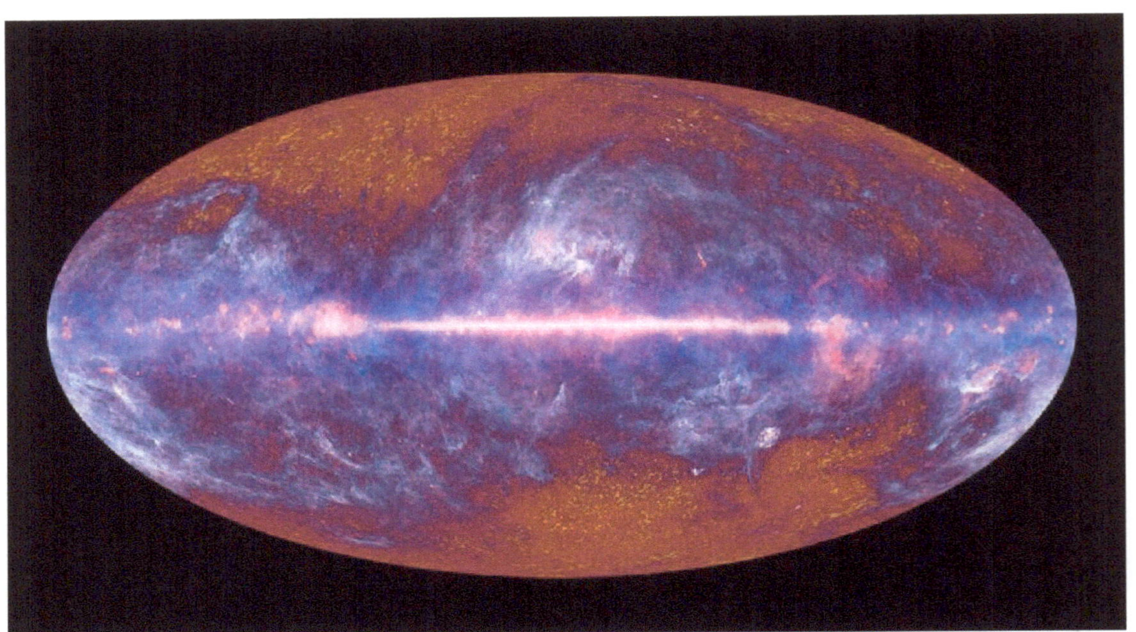

The Cosmic Microwave Background (CMB) is the cooled remnant of the first light that could ever travel freely throughout the Universe. This 'fossil' radiation, the furthest that any telescope can see, was released soon after the 'Big Bang'. Scientists consider it as an echo or 'shockwave' of the Big Bang.

Dance of venus and earth:

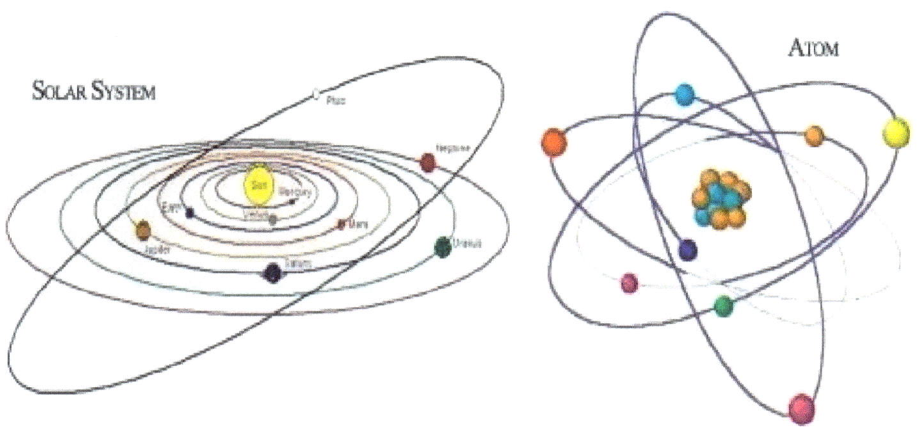

DIAGRAM OF THE SOLAR SYSTEM AS COMPARED TO THAT OF AN ATOM

THE ELECTROMAGNETIC SPECTRUM

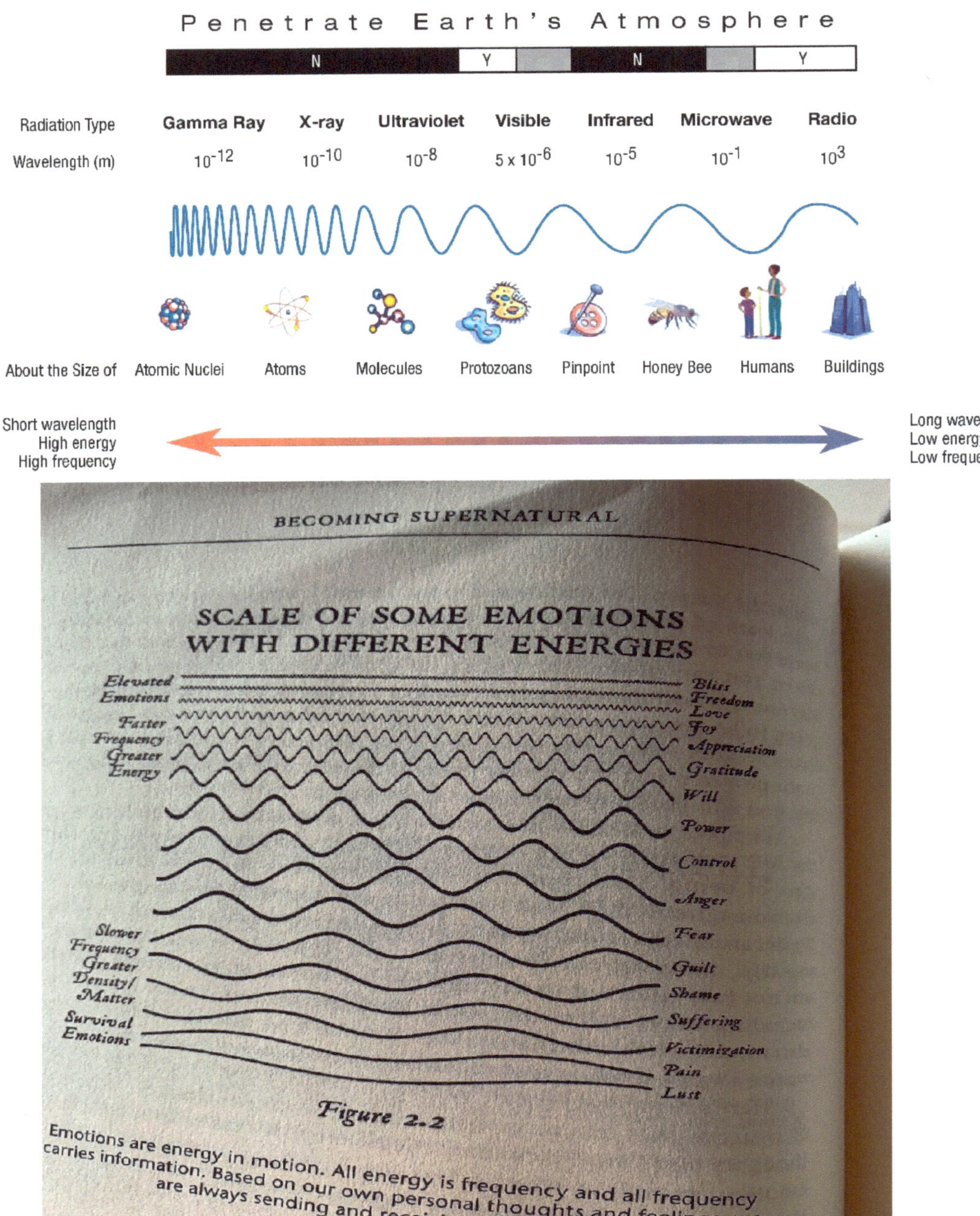

Emotions are energy in motion. All energy is frequency and all frequency carries information. Based on our own personal thoughts and feelings, we are always sending and receiving information from the Universe.

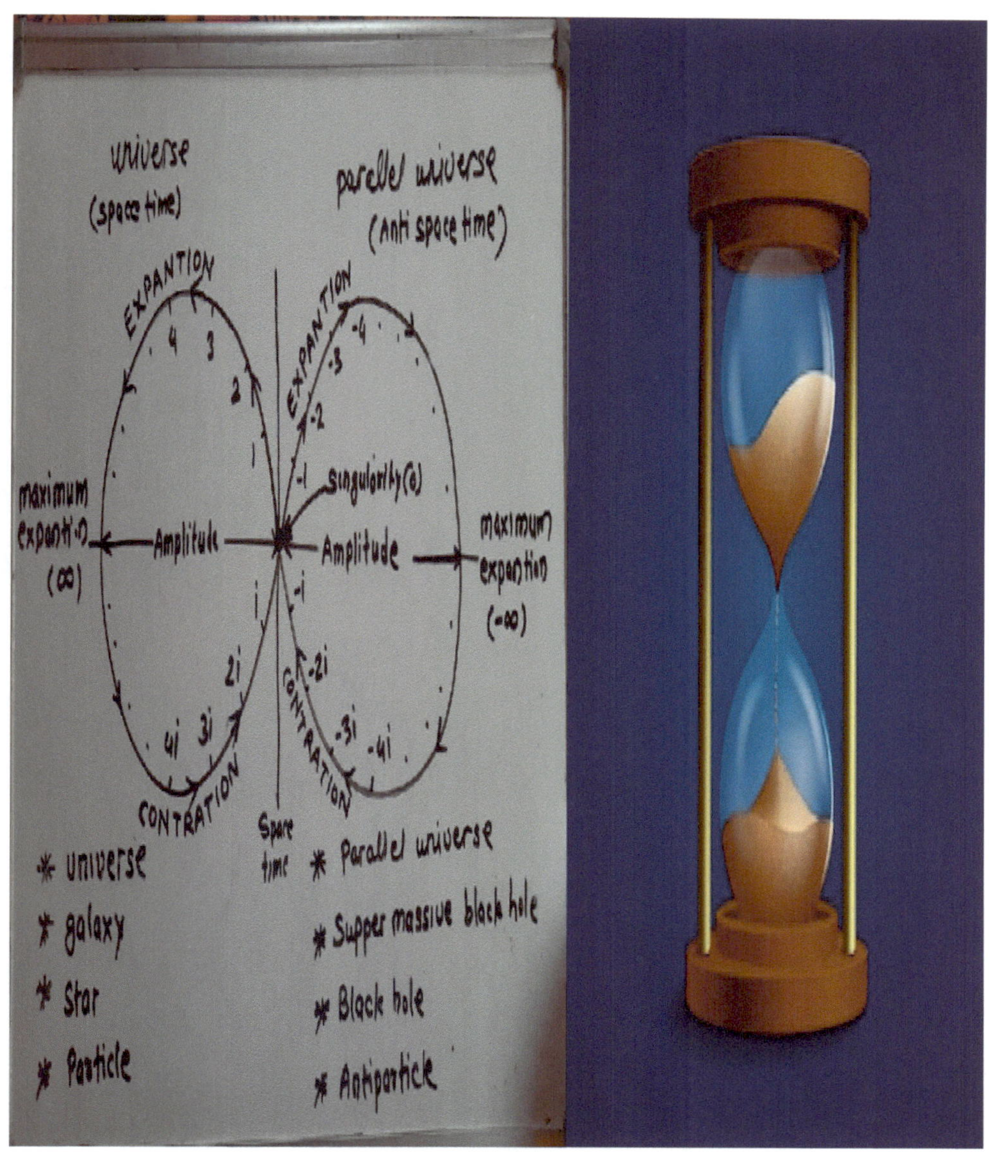

parallel universe

Big Bang Theory

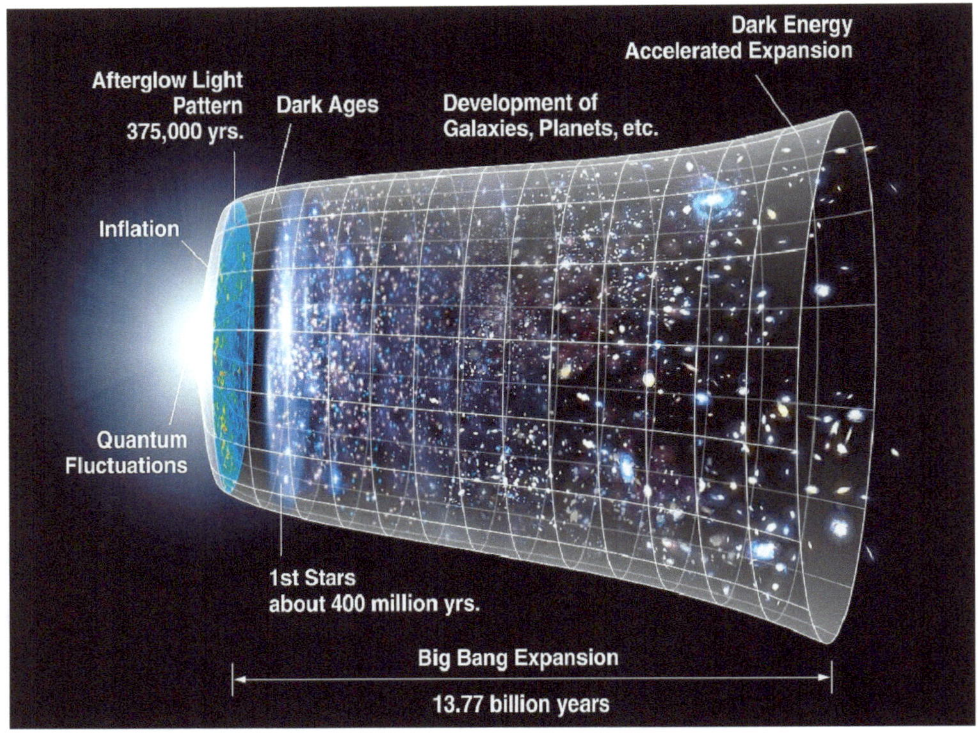

Around 13.7 billion years ago, everything in the entire universe was condensed in an infinitesimally small singularity, a point of infinite denseness and heat. Suddenly, an explosive expansion began, ballooning our universe outwards faster than the speed of light. This was a period of cosmic inflation that lasted mere fractions of a second — about 10^{-32} of a second, according to physicist Alan Guth's 1980 theory that changed the way we think about the Big Bang forever. When cosmic inflation came to a sudden and still-mysterious end, the more classic descriptions of the Big Bang took hold. A flood of matter and radiation, known as "reheating," began populating our universe with the stuff we know today: particles, atoms, the stuff that would become stars and galaxies and so on. This all happened within just the first second after the universe began, when the temperature of everything was still insanely hot, at about 10 billion degrees Fahrenheit (5.5 billion Celsius), according to NASA.

The cosmos now contained a vast array of fundamental particles such as neutrons, electrons and protons — the raw materials that would become the building blocks for everything that exists todayThis early "soup" would have been impossible to actually see because it couldn't hold visible light. "The free electrons would have caused light (photons) to scatter the way sunlight scatters from the water droplets in clouds," NASA stated. Over time, however, these free electrons met up with nuclei and created neutral atoms or atoms with equal positive and negative electric charges. This allowed light to finally shine through, about 380,000 years after the Big Bang.Sometimes called the "afterglow" of the Big Bang, this light is more properly known as the cosmic microwave background (CMB). It was first predicted by Ralph Alpher and other scientists in 1948 but was found only by accident almost 20 years later.This accidental discovery happened when Arno Penzias and Robert Wilson, both of Bell Telephone Laboratories in New Jersey, were building a radio receiver in 1965 and picked up higher-than-expected temperatures, according to a NASA article. At first, they thought the anomaly was due to pigeons trying to roost inside the antenna and their waste, but they cleaned up the mess and killed the pigeons and the anomaly persisted.Simultaneously, a Princeton University team led by Robert Dicke was trying to find evidence of the CMB and realized that Penzias and Wilson had stumbled upon it with their strange observations. The two groups each published papers in the Astrophysical Journal in 1965. to reach the first instant after the Big Bang by simulating 4,000 versions of the current universe on a massive supercomputer. "We are trying to do something like guessing a baby photo of our universe from the latest picture," study leader Masato Shirasaki, a cosmologist at the National Astronomical Observatory of Japan (NAOJ), wrote in an email to our sister website Live Science. With what is known about the universe today, the researchers in this 2021 study compared their understanding of how gravitational forces interacted in the primordial universe with their thousands of computer-modeled universes.

If they could predict the starting conditions of their virtual universes, they hoped to be able to accurately predict what our own universe may have looked like back at the beginning. Other researchers have chosen different paths to interrogate our universe's beginnings. In a 2020 study, researchers did so by investigating the split between matter and antimatter. In the study, not yet peer-reviewed, they proposed that the imbalance in the amount of matter and antimatter in the universe is related to the universe's vast quantities of dark matter, an unknown substance that exerts influence over gravity and yet doesn't interact with light. They suggested that in the crucial moments immediately after the Big Bang, the universe may have been pushed to make more matter than its inverse, antimatter, which then could have led to the formation of dark matter

THE AGE OF THE UNIVERSE-The CMB has been observed by many researchers now and with many spacecraft missions. One of the most famous space-faring missions to do so was NASA's Cosmic Background Explorer (COBE) satellite, which mapped the sky in the 1990s.Several other missions have followed in COBE's footsteps, such as the BOOMERanG experiment (Balloon Observations of Millimetric Extragalactic Radiation and Geophysics), NASA's Wilkinson Microwave Anisotropy Probe (WMAP) and the European Space Agency's Planck satellite.Planck's observations, first released in 2013, mapped the CMB in unprecedented detail and revealed that the universe was older than previously thought: 13.82 billion years old, rather than 13.7 billion years old. The research observatory's mission is ongoing and new maps of the CMB are released periodically.The maps give rise to new mysteries, however, such as why the Southern Hemisphere appears slightly redder (warmer) than the Northern Hemisphere. The Big Bang Theory says that the CMB would be mostly the same, no matter where you look.Examining the CMB also gives astronomers clues as to the composition of the universe. Researchers think most of the cosmos is made up of matter and energy that cannot be "sensed" with our conventional instruments, leading to the names "dark matter" and "dark energy."It is thought that only 5% of the universe is made up of matter such as planets, stars and galaxies.

While astronomers study the universe's beginnings through creative measures and mathematical simulations, they've also been seeking proof of its rapid inflation. They have done this by studying gravitational waves, tiny perturbations in space-time that ripple outwards from great disturbances like, for instance, two black holes colliding, or the birth of the universe.According to leading theories, in the first second after the universe was born, our cosmos ballooned faster than the speed of light. (That, by the way, does not violate Albert Einstein's speed limit. He once said that light speed is the fastest anything can travel within the universe — but that statement did not apply to the inflation of the universe itself.)As the universe expanded, it created the CMB and a similar "background noise" made up of gravitational waves that, like the CMB, were a sort of static, detectable from all parts of the sky. Those gravitational waves, according to the LIGO Scientific Collaboration, produced a theorized barely-detectable polarization, one type of which is called "B-modes."In 2014, astronomers said they had found evidence of B-modes using an Antarctic telescope called "Background Imaging of Cosmic Extragalactic Polarization," or BICEP2."We're very confident that the signal that we're seeing is real, and it's on the sky," lead researcher John Kovac, of the Harvard-Smithsonian Center for Astrophysics, told Space.com in March 2014.But by June, the same team said that their findings could have been altered by galactic dust getting in the way of their field of view. That hypothesis was supported by new results from the Planck satellite.By January 2015, researchers from both teams working together "confirmed that the Bicep signal was mostly, if not all, stardust," the New York Times saidHowever, since then gravitational waves have not only been confirmed to exist, they have been observed multiple times. These waves, which are not B-modes from the birth of the universe but rather from more recent collisions of black holes, have been detected multiple times by the Laser Interferometer Gravitational-Wave Observatory (LIGO), with the first-ever gravitational wave detection taking place in 2016.

As LIGO becomes more sensitive, it is anticipated that discovering black hole-related gravitational waves will be a fairly frequent event.

WAS THE BIG BANG AN EXPLOSION?

Although the Big Bang is often described as an "explosion", that's a misleading image. In an explosion, fragments are flung out from a central point into a pre-existing space. If you were at the central point, you'd see all the fragments moving away from you at roughly the same speed. But the Big Bang wasn't like that. It was an expansion of space itself – a concept that comes out of Einstein's equations of general relativity but has no counterpart in the classical physics of everyday life. It means that all the distances in the universe are stretching out at the same rate. Any two galaxies separated by distance X are receding from each other at the same speed, while a galaxy at distance 2X recedes at twice that speed.

THE UNIVERSE'S CONTINUED EXPANSION

The universe is not only expanding, but expanding faster. This means that with time, nobody will be able to spot other galaxies from Earth or any other vantage point within our galaxy."We will see distant galaxies moving away from us, but their speed is increasing with time," Harvard University astronomer Avi Loeb said in a March 2014 Space.com article."So, if you wait long enough, eventually, a distant galaxy will reach the speed of light. What that means is that even light won't be able to bridge the gap that's being opened between that galaxy and us. There's no way for extraterrestrials on that galaxy to communicate with us, to send any signals that will reach us, once their galaxy is moving faster than light relative to us."Some physicists also suggest that the universe we experience is just one of many. In the "multiverse" model, different universes would coexist with each other like bubbles lying side by side. The theory suggests that in that first big push of inflation, different parts of space-time grew at different rates.

This could have carved off different sections — different universes — with potentially different laws of physics."It's hard to build models of inflation that don't lead to a multiverse," Alan Guth, a theoretical physicist at the Massachusetts Institute of Technology, said during a news conference in March 2014 concerning the gravitational waves discovery. (Guth is not affiliated with that study.)"It's not impossible, so I think there's still certainly research that needs to be done. But most models of inflation do lead to a multiverse, and evidence for inflation will be pushing us in the direction of taking [the idea of a] multiverse seriously."While we can understand how the universe we see came to be, it's possible that the Big Bang was not the first inflationary period the universe experienced. Some scientists believe we live in a cosmos that goes through regular cycles of inflation and deflation, and that we just happen to be living in one of these phases.

JWST AND THE BIG BANG

A telescope is almost like a time machine, allowing us to peer back into the distant past. With the aid of the Hubble space telescope, NASA has shown us galaxies as they were many billions of years ago — and Hubble's successor, the James Webb Space Telescope, has the ability to look even deeper into the past. NASA hopes it will see all the way back to when the first galaxies formed, nearly 13.6 billion years ago. And unlike Hubble, which sees mainly in the visible waveband, JWST is an infrared telescope — a big advantage when looking at very distant galaxies. The expansion of the universe means that waves emitted from them are stretched out, so light that was emitted at visible wavelengths actually reaches us in the infrared.

THE BIG BANG THEORY: The name "Big Bang Theory" has been a popular way to talk about the concept among astrophysicists for decades, but it hit the mainstream in 2007 when a comedy T.V. show with the same name premiered on CBS. Running for 279 episodes over 12 seasons, the show "The Big Bang Theory" followed the lives of a group of scientists, which included physicists, astrophysicists and aerospace engineers. The show explores the group's nerdy friendships, romances and squabbles. Its first season premiered on Sept. 24, 2007, and the show officially ended on May 16, 2019.Although the show itself didn't dive too much into actual science, the showrunners did hire UCLA astrophysicist David Saltzberg as a science consultant for the entire run of the show, according to Science magazine. Science consultants are often hired for sci-fi and science-related shows and movies to help keep certain aspects realistic.Thanks to Saltzberg, the characters' vocabulary included a host of science jargon and the whiteboards in the background of labs, offices and apartments throughout the show were filled with a variety of equations and information. Over the course of the show, Saltzberg said, those whiteboards became coveted space as researchers sent him new work that they hoped might be featured there. In one episode, Saltzberg recalled, new evidence of gravitational waves was scrawled across a whiteboard that ostensibly belonged to famed physicist Steven Hawking, who also approved the text.Notably, several characters in the series take trips. One episode sees main characters Leonard, Sheldon, Raj and Howard set out on a research expedition to the Arctic — many physics experiments are best performed at or near the extreme environments of the poles. Another put aerospace engineer Howard on a Russian Soyuz spacecraft and, later, a model of the International Space Station along witA black hole is a volume of space where gravity is so strong that nothing, not even light, can escape from it. This astonishing idea was first announced in 1783 by John Michell, real-life astronaut Mike Massimino.

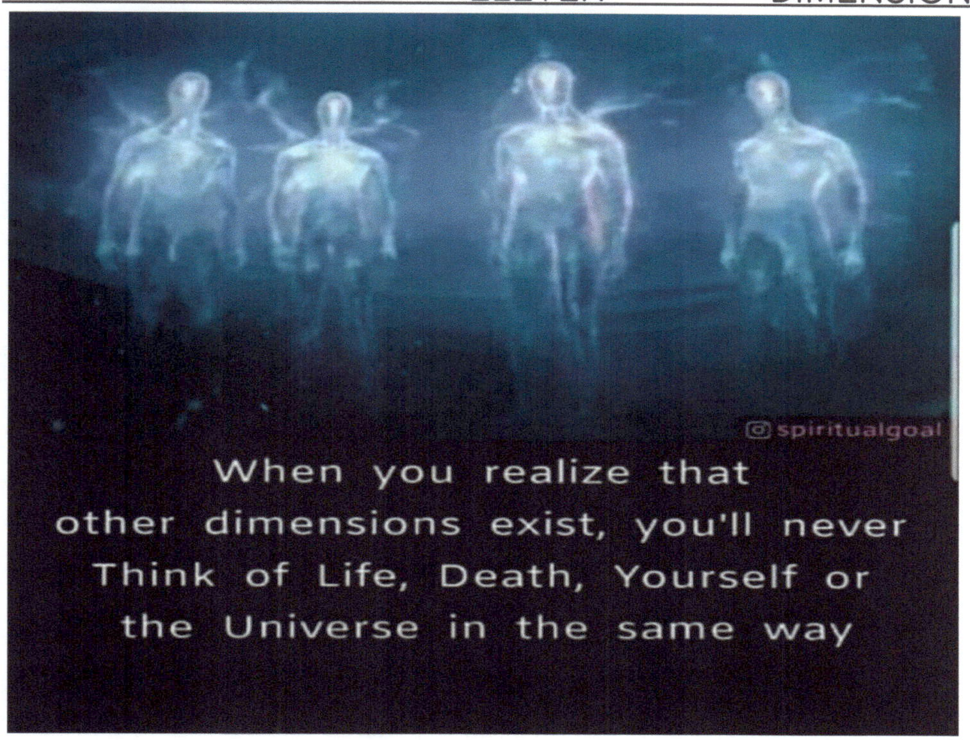
spiritualgoal
When you realize that
other dimensions exist, you'll never
Think of Life, Death, Yourself or
the Universe in the same way

QUANTUM THEORY

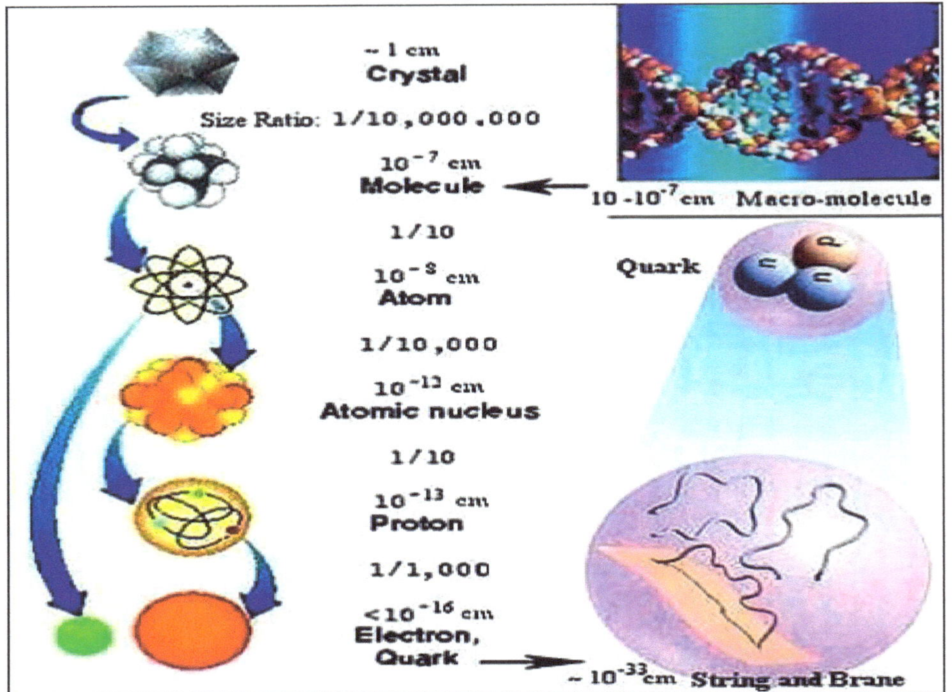

- Quantum theory is the theoretical basis of modern physics that explains the nature and behavior of matter and energy on the atomic and subatomic level. The nature and behavior of matter and energy at that level is sometimes referred to as quantum physics and quantum mechanics.

- Planck length=The Planck length is the scale at which classi-cal ideas about gravity and space-time cease to be valid, and quantum effects dominate. This is the 'quantum of length', the smallest measurement of length with any meaning. And roughly equal to 1.6×10^{-35} m or about 10^{-20} times the size of a proton.

- The number 137, according to Lederman, "shows up naked all over the place", meaning that scientists on any planet in the universe using whatever units they have for charge or speed, and whatever their version of Planck's constant may be, will all come up with 137, because it is a pure number

The Modern Science is an excellent solution for current issues. But here, one has to think of Entropy. What is entropy. To make coffee, one has to mix milk, sugar and coffee powder. The World we see Today is just like a Coffee. We cannot reverse the coffee to its ingredients. Here Modern Science fails. That's why it can not tell what happened before Big Bang . (The age of the universe is the time elapsed since the Big Bang is 13.8 billion years old.)

An attempt has been made in writing this book is to create clues to search the God/Creator. If any one , who interested to found the Creator, this book may be used as Reference.

CHAPTER 4
UN ANSWERED QUESTION/MYSTERIES

- What is the purpose of life?
- How big is the universe?
- Where did everything come from?
- What came first the chicken or the egg?
- What happens after we die? Does our soul continue after death or is death the end?
- Does God exist? If God made everything who made God?
- Are there other beings out there?
- Exactly how long will I live?
- Is time travel possible?
- If there are aliens, where are they?
- Why do girls have more cells than boys?
- What is consciousness?

IN SEARCH OF GOD BY GOPALA KRISHNA MERUVA